APR 2 2 1995

HILLSDALE BRANCH

D0646266

GREAT
Presidential
DECISIONS

The Jefferson Way

JEFFREY MORRIS

LERNER PUBLICATIONS COMPANY
MINNEAPOLIS

Public Library San Mateo, CA

To David,
who brings joy to our lives

Copyright © 1994 Jeffrey B. Morris
Published by arrangement with Lou Reda Productions, Inc.

All rights reserved. International copyright secured. No part
of this book may be reproduced, stored in a retrieval system,
or transmitted in any form or by any means, electronic,
mechanical, photocopying, recording, or otherwise, without
the prior written permission of Lerner Publications Company,
except for the inclusion of brief quotations in an
acknowledged review.

Library of Congress Cataloging-in-Publication Data

Morris, Jeffrey Brandon, 1941-
    The Jefferson way / by Jeffrey B. Morris
        p. cm. — (Great presidential decisions)
    Includes index.
    ISBN 0-8225-2926-2
    1. Jefferson, Thomas, 1743-1826—Juvenile literature. 2. United
States—Politics and government—1783-1809—Juvenile literature.
[1. Jefferson, Thomas, 1743-1826. 2. Presidents. 3. United
States—Politics and government—1783-1809.] I. Title. II. Series.
E332.79.M585 1994
973.4'6—dc20   94-923
                                                            CIP
                                                            AC

Manufactured in the United States of America
    1 2 3 4 5 6 – I/JR – 99 98 97 96 95 94

Contents

Introduction

*T*HE AMERICANS WHO WROTE the Constitution of the United States faced an unusual opportunity. They wanted to give American presidents enough power to make important decisions but not enough power to become a monarch. They wanted to protect the rights of citizens by limiting the power of the president.

Their country had won independence from Great Britain, which had a monarchical government. Most European nations at that time were governed by monarchies—by kings and queens. But Americans wanted a republic, a form of government in which power resides with those citizens who are entitled to vote. The government is run by elected officers and representatives who are responsible to the citizenry and who govern according to law.

The signing of the Constitution, presented here by artist Thomas Rossiter, took place on September 17, 1787, at the Pennsylvania State House (now called Independence Hall) in Philadelphia, Pennsylvania.

Because of his speeches, negotiations, and attempts at compromise during the Constitutional Convention, James Madison became known as the Father of the Constitution. Madison told the delegates they were considering a plan that "would decide forever the fate of republican government." He also kept a record of the debates and decisions of the delegates.

The framers of the United States Constitution wanted a government powerful enough to protect the country from foreign enemies, but not powerful enough to take away the rights of the citizens. To accomplish this goal, they created a complex form of government. The framers divided the powers of the new government among three branches. They thought that the least powerful branch would be the judiciary. That branch was supposed to hear and decide lawsuits, decide disputes between the U.S. government and individual states, and keep the other two branches within their constitutional powers.

The framers expected the legislative branch—the Senate and the House of Representatives—to be the most powerful. Congress was supposed to make laws, levy taxes, and choose how to spend money.

The framers of the Constitution had the most trouble agreeing on the powers of the executive branch. The head of that branch is the president. The framers wanted a president who could act speedily and forcefully. On the other hand, they definitely did not want someone with the powers of a king or dictator. The president would be elected for four years. He or she would be commander in chief of the military forces, would be primarily responsible for relations with other countries, and would ensure that the laws passed by Congress would be carried out. The president could also veto laws passed by Congress, but Congress could override that veto.

The framers thought that each branch of government would work at a different rate of speed, because each would have its own set of duties. They thought the judicial branch would act most slowly, partly because lawyers usually need time to gather evidence and present their case, and because fair decisions require careful deliberation. The framers of the Constitution thought Congress would also act relatively slowly, because of the need to gather information, debate the issues, and get agreement among many members. The framers, however, wanted the president to be able to act rapidly and decisively.

When they drafted the Constitution, the framers expected that Congress and the Supreme Court would meet at the nation's capital for only a few months each year. But they intended that the president, even if he was away from the capital, would act for the nation in an emergency. The framers also wanted to be sure that in some areas—such as dealing with other nations—the United States should be as unified as possible, and they hoped that the president would express that unity. For these reasons—speed, unity, and the ability to act in an emergency—the framers expected that the president would often be called upon to make important decisions.

George Washington speaks to delegates at the Constitutional Convention in Philadelphia, Pennsylvania.

This series is about the great decisions that some of our presidents made. Of course, presidents make decisions every day. They decide whom to appoint to office, what to say to leaders of foreign nations, whether or not to veto laws passed by Congress. Most of these decisions are quite ordinary. From time to time, however, the president makes a decision that will affect the American people (and often other nations as well) for many years, maybe even centuries. You may think of Abraham Lincoln's decision to free the slaves, or Franklin Roosevelt's decision to fight the Great Depression, or John Kennedy's decision to fight for civil rights for African Americans. Of course, not every important decision our presidents

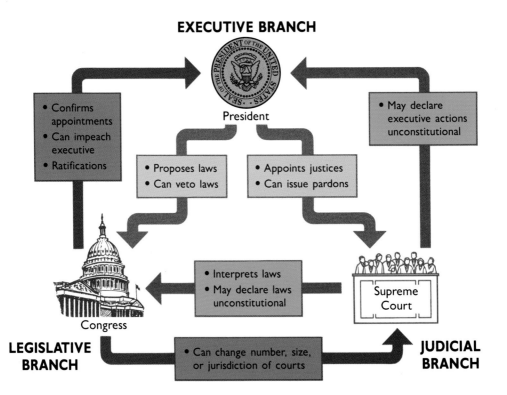

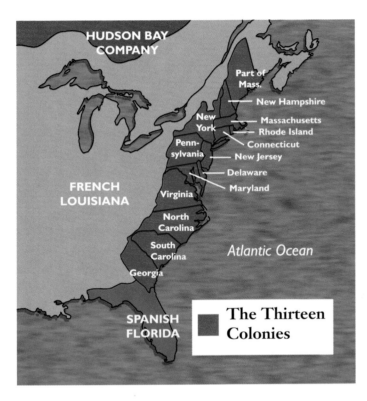

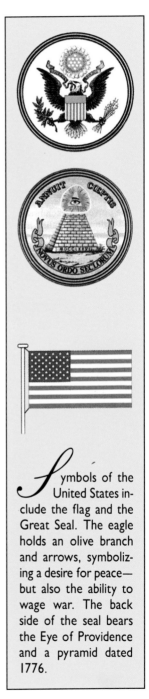

have made has been wise. James Buchanan decided not to stop the Southern states from leaving the Union. Franklin Roosevelt decided to ask Congress to increase the size of the Supreme Court so it would more often decide cases the way he wanted. Richard Nixon decided to cover up the Watergate burglary.

This book is about the decisions made by Thomas Jefferson, the third president, and one of the greatest Americans. Two of Jefferson's decisions worked out well, but two others did not. You'll find out what led to his decisions, the options he had at the time, and how he actually went about making decisions. You'll also see how his decisions were carried out and why they were important.

*S*ymbols of the United States include the flag and the Great Seal. The eagle holds an olive branch and arrows, symbolizing a desire for peace—but also the ability to wage war. The back side of the seal bears the Eye of Providence and a pyramid dated 1776.

Starting Out

*S*HORTLY BEFORE NOON ON March 4, 1801, a tall, redheaded, 57-year-old man with a freckled face walked about 200 feet from his boardinghouse in Washington, D.C., to the building that housed the U.S. Congress. That building was not the magnificent structure with the great, white dome that currently commands Capitol Hill. Indeed, the hill itself was then known as Jenkins Hill. The day Thomas Jefferson was inaugurated as the third president of the United States, the Congress was housed in a single white stone building.

The Inauguration of 1801

Jefferson's inauguration ceremony was simple—far more so than the inaugurations of George Washing-

Thomas Jefferson was the first president to be inaugurated in Washington, D.C. Here he is dismounting from his horse to attend his inauguration in the new Capitol in 1801.

This is an early view of the Capitol in Washington, D.C. The House of Representatives was connected to the Senate by a passageway—where the Rotunda now stands. When Jefferson took office, only the right wing had been completed.

ton and John Adams. A company of riflemen from Alexandria, Virginia, marched with drawn swords. Jefferson walked behind them, accompanied by members of Congress and other friends. When he arrived at the Capitol, the riflemen opened ranks and saluted. Jefferson then entered the room housing the Senate, and everyone rose. He took his place in the center chair at the front of the room. On his left was the chief justice of the United States, John Marshall. On his right was the new vice president, Aaron

Burr, who, at five feet, five inches, was more than half a foot shorter than the other two men. Missing from the ceremony was the man Jefferson had defeated for the presidency, John Adams. Adams had gotten up in the middle of the night and left the White House at four in the morning to avoid attending the inauguration.

Jefferson rose to give his inaugural address. He was not a good speaker—only some of those in the crowded Senate chamber could hear him. When he was finished, the chief justice administered the oath of office. Immediately afterward, the Alexandria company fired a 16-round salute. With no further fanfare, President Jefferson walked back to his boardinghouse and began to work.

Aaron Burr became vice president in 1801.

Although the ceremony had been simple, it was significant. Indeed, Thomas Jefferson's inauguration in 1801 may have been the most important one in American history. For the very first time, one political party (the Federalists) surrendered its power peacefully to another (the Democratic-Republicans) because they had lost an election. Even now in many parts of the world, power changes hands only through revolution or military takeover. On March 4, 1801, Margaret Bayard Smith, the wife of a Washington newspaper editor, knew the importance of what she had seen. In a letter to her sister-in-law, she wrote:

> I have this morning witnessed one of the most interesting scenes a free people can ever witness. The changes of administration, which in every government and in every age have most generally been epochs of confusion, villainy and bloodshed, in this our happy country take place without any species of distraction or disorder.

John Adams, a Federalist, disagreed with many of Jefferson's political ideals.

A pencil sketch of Thomas Jefferson, drawn about 1799

A Man of Many Talents

No American, with the possible exception of Benjamin Franklin, had such a range of abilities as Jefferson. Biographer James Parton described Jefferson as "a gentleman of 32 who could calculate an eclipse, survey an estate, tie an artery, plan an edifice, break a horse, dance a minuet." He could speak four languages (English, French, Spanish, and Italian) and could also read Greek and Latin. He was as well read as anyone in America, and he owned the best library. He also wrote very well. It was said of Jefferson that he "could put words together and fashion them into a powerful weapon." Among U.S. presidents, only Abraham Lincoln (and possibly Woodrow Wilson) was Jefferson's equal with a pen. Although Jefferson never became famous as a lawyer, he had shown in Virginia's House of Burgesses that he was probably the leading reformer of law in America.

But there was more. As an architectural engineer, he helped design Washington, D.C., and the University of Virginia. He was also an educator and one of the leading American scientists of his day. He made important contributions to paleontology (the study of fossils), botany (the study of flowers and plants), and meteorology (the study of weather).

There is a story—whether true or not—that once when traveling in Virginia, Jefferson stopped in a country inn and got into a conversation with a stranger. The stranger mentioned some mechanical operation he had recently seen, and Jefferson's knowledge of the subject convinced the man that Jefferson was an engineer. Then they began talking about agriculture, and the stranger decided Jefferson was a farmer. More talk led the stranger to believe that Jefferson was a lawyer, then a doctor. Finally, the topic changed to religion, and the stranger was convinced that Jefferson was a minister—although he wasn't sure of which religion. The following day, the stranger asked the innkeeper the name of the tall man he had talked with the night before. "Why, that was President Jefferson," said the innkeeper.

The Early Years

*T*HOMAS JEFFERSON WAS BORN IN a four-room wooden house at Shadwell, one of his father's tobacco plantations. Shadwell was in the western part of Virginia, which was then very wild. Wolves, bears, and panthers lived in the woods near Tom's home. Because there were no public schools in those days, Tom had tutors who came to his home. Later he went to boarding school.

Tom's father, Peter Jefferson, was a wealthy man. It was said that he was so strong he could lift two 1,000-pound hogsheads (barrels) of tobacco to an upright position at the same time. Tom's mother, Jane Randolph Jefferson, came from one of the oldest families in Virginia. Tom was the third child in a

The Second Continental Congress adopted the Declaration of Independence on July 4, 1776. In this painting, John Hancock, president of the Congress, sits at the right. Standing in front of him, *from left to right,* are John Adams, Roger Sherman, Robert Livingston, Thomas Jefferson, and Benjamin Franklin, the committee that drafted the Declaration.

George Wythe was a distinguished lawyer and judge in the state of Virginia. He was appointed to the nation's first law professorship, which was established in 1779 at the College of William and Mary. The college was founded in 1693.

family of 10 children. He was 14 when his father died, and he inherited more than 2,500 acres of his father's land.

When Tom was almost 17, he traveled to Williamsburg, which was then the capital of Virginia. There he attended the College of William and Mary for two years. Although Tom excelled in many of his courses, he was particularly interested in mathematics, architecture, and music. When he graduated from college, however, he chose to stay in Williamsburg and study with George Wythe, America's first great teacher of law. Jefferson practiced law for a few years, but it never interested him as much as politics and farming did.

At that time in Virginia, wealthy landowners often became political leaders. In 1769, when he was 26 years old, Jefferson was elected to the Virginia House of Burgesses, part of the legislative branch of Virginia's government. There he met and became friends with George Washington, Judge Edmund Pendleton, Patrick Henry, and James Madison.

The years from 1769 to 1776 were busy years for Jefferson. Besides sitting in the House of Burgesses, practicing law, and running his plantations, he met and married Martha Wayles Skelton. They had six children, although only two daughters, Martha and Maria, lived to adulthood.

In 1769 Jefferson began a project that he continued throughout most of his life—building a beautiful home overlooking the countryside. He called this home Monticello, which means "little mountain" in Italian. From Monticello, Jefferson could see the Blue Ridge Mountains to the west and the dense forests that stretched to the east. The town of Charlottesville was to the north, while to the south was another larger mountain.

Jefferson not only designed Monticello but also acted as engineer, construction foreman, cabinetmaker, and landscaper. The main house, a three-story building with 35 rooms, was not completed until 1809. One of its impressive features was a domed, octagonal room. Passageways connected two long terraces above the kitchen, dairy, laundry, icehouse, carriage house, and stables. Monticello also had all sorts of gadgets, including a dumbwaiter, a table with a top that could be raised and lowered, an octagonal filing table, a four-sided, revolving bookstand made of walnut, and a clock that had cannonballs as weights.

While Jefferson continued working on Monticello, tensions had been growing between Great Britain and the American colonies. At first, Jefferson had been an observer in the House of Burgesses, but he soon joined those with bolder views—men like George Washington and Patrick Henry. He helped create "committees of correspondence," which were networks for exchanging information and developing common actions among the colonies. Jefferson was never a great orator like Patrick Henry, but he was a superb writer—and his fellow burgesses recognized his talent. When *A Summary View of the Rights of British America*, a 23-page pamphlet, was published in 1774, patriots all over America learned who the author was—although Jefferson's name did not appear on it. The pamphlet was a statement of colonial grievances against the British government, and it made Jefferson a champion of freedom and self-government.

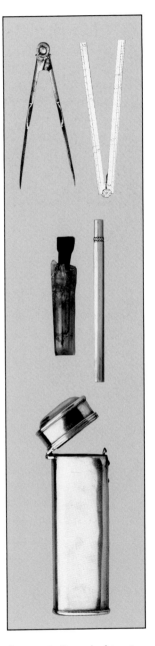

A set of silver drafting instruments owned and used by Jefferson

To the right is a view of Monticello, Jefferson's beloved home in Virginia. Below is the reception hall, which features one of the most spectacular of Jefferson's inventions. He designed a seven-day clock that also tells the days of the week with cannonball weights descending past placards indicating the days of the week. The antlers hanging on the wall were brought back by explorers Lewis and Clark from their western expedition.

Benjamin Franklin, Thomas Jefferson, John Adams, Robert Livingston, and Roger Sherman meet to plan the Declaration of Independence, *left*.

Jefferson's Career

In 1775 Jefferson was chosen as a delegate from Virginia to the Second Continental Congress, which met in Philadelphia. This was his debut as a national political leader. A year later, his fellow congressmen elected him to a committee to prepare a declaration of independence. His fellow committee members— Benjamin Franklin, John Adams, Roger Sherman, and Robert R. Livingston—asked Jefferson to prepare the first draft. Working for 17 days, from June 11 to June 28, 1776, Jefferson produced a draft that Franklin and Adams changed only slightly. Much to Jefferson's annoyance, however, the Continental Congress made a considerable number of changes. Most were unimportant, and some were improvements.

A rotating book stand designed by Jefferson

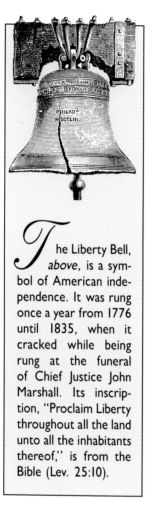

The Liberty Bell, *above*, is a symbol of American independence. It was rung once a year from 1776 until 1835, when it cracked while being rung at the funeral of Chief Justice John Marshall. Its inscription, "Proclaim Liberty throughout all the land unto all the inhabitants thereof," is from the Bible (Lev. 25:10).

Jefferson was particularly disturbed when Congress, deferring to the delegates from South Carolina and Georgia, dropped a provision that denounced the British king, George III, for allowing the slave trade to continue.

Nevertheless, the great opening paragraphs of the Declaration of Independence were almost entirely Jefferson's words, including the most famous lines:

> We hold these truths to be self-evident, that all men are created equal, that they are endowed by their Creator with certain unalienable Rights, that among these are Life, Liberty and the pursuit of Happiness. That to secure these rights, Governments are instituted among Men, deriving their just Powers from the consent of the governed.

But the Declaration of Independence was not the only important document that Jefferson wrote. As a legislator, Jefferson fought to separate church and state. In 1779 Jefferson drafted the *Virginia Statute of Religious Freedom*, which became law in 1786. It completely separated church and state and placed religious beliefs beyond the jurisdiction, or control, of government. This landmark document set the pattern governing church-state relations in the United States. It declared that no one could be forced to attend or pay for any church, and that it was illegal to discriminate against someone because of his or her religious beliefs.

A Change in Plans

When his beloved wife, Martha, died in 1782, Jefferson no longer felt happy at Monticello. He agreed to succeed Benjamin Franklin as U.S. minister to

To the left is a draft of the Declaration of Independence. As you can see, Jefferson made many revisions. In this section, he addresses the injustice of slavery. Like other plantation owners of his day, however, Jefferson owned slaves.

The Marquis de Lafayette, a French soldier and statesman, helped the American colonists in the Revolutionary War. He became a major general in the American army and persuaded France to send military aid to the colonists. Lafayette also assisted in the negotiations that won American independence.

France. Jefferson spent five years in Paris, and with growing excitement, he watched the power of the king and the aristocracy weaken. The author of the Declaration of Independence was in Paris on July 14, 1789, when Parisians stormed the fortress known as the Bastille and began the French Revolution. Throughout the summer of 1789, Jefferson met with the Marquis de Lafayette, the French hero of the American Revolution, and other liberal aristocrats to advise them about forming a plan of government and drafting a French declaration of rights.

In the meantime, Americans were creating their own constitution. Although Jefferson was 3,000 miles away from Philadelphia, his old friend James Madison played a major role at the Constitutional Convention. When Jefferson first saw a draft of the Constitution in November 1787, he was not enthusiastic. Jefferson objected to the absence of both a bill of rights and a ban on the reelection of the president. By July 1788, however, he had overcome his

During the summer of 1789, the middle and lower classes rebelled against the power of the king and the privileges of the aristocrats and the clergy. On July 14, a huge crowd of workers captured the Bastille, a prison and a symbol of hated political power, *right*.

Market Street in Philadelphia, 1799. Jefferson's residence is in the right foreground.

Secretary of the Treasury Alexander Hamilton, *top*, and Secretary of State Thomas Jefferson, *bottom*. Although they were both great statesmen, they disagreed philosophically.

objections and wrote to Madison: "It is a good canvas, on which some strokes only want retouching."

Jefferson came back to America in the winter of 1789. He thought his visit would be brief, but President George Washington appointed him secretary of state in the new government.

As secretary of state, Jefferson was responsible for the country's relationships with other nations, but always under the close supervision of the president. In those days the Department of State was also responsible for an assortment of other duties, because Congress had not quite known whose jurisdiction to put them under. For example, Jefferson was responsible for supervising the first census and for granting patents and copyrights. Furthermore, when Jefferson became secretary of state, he had only two clerks

President George Washington, *far left,* and his cabinet: *from left to right,* Secretary of War Henry Knox, Secretary of the Treasury Alexander Hamilton, Secretary of State Thomas Jefferson, Attorney General Edmund Randolph

working for him. Congress later provided him with three more clerks, a part-time interpreter, a doorkeeper, and a messenger—quite a contrast to the number of workers in federal departments nowadays.

After almost four years as secretary of state, Jefferson became tired of the battles he was having with Secretary of the Treasury Alexander Hamilton—battles Hamilton seemed to be winning more and more often. Jefferson, who wanted the United States to remain a nation of farmers, disagreed with Hamilton's plans to encourage shipping and manufacturing. He also opposed Hamilton's plan to establish a national bank, because he believed it would give the government too much power. Washington, how-

John Adams, *left,* seldom achieved popularity during his long political career. Although he was not a cold man, his bluntness, impatience, and vanity probably made more enemies than friends. During Adams's term as president, the United States took its first steps toward industrialization. The first woolen mills began operating in Massachusetts, and Congress established the Department of the Navy and the Marine Corps.

ever, sided with Hamilton. On the last day of 1793, Jefferson resigned as secretary of state, expecting to spend the rest of his life at Monticello.

However, when he was elected vice president of the United States in 1796, Jefferson once again left Monticello for Philadelphia. The president was his old friend John Adams, but the political events of the next few years interrupted their friendship.

The Election of 1800:
A Divided America

*T*HE 1790s WERE AMONG THE MOST contentious years in the history of American politics. Eleven years of quarreling over government policies had caused a division among Americans that led to the development of political parties. The Federalists, led by Alexander Hamilton and John Adams, believed in a strong national government and a strong presidency. They wanted the government to play an active role in encouraging shipping, commerce, and industry, and they mistrusted the ability of the people to govern.

Jefferson's Democratic-Republican Party believed that the people, acting through elected representatives, could be left to govern themselves. The Democratic-

Democratic elections were an important feature of the new nation's Constitution. In Philadelphia flags waved and many people turned out to vote on election day.

*A*lexander Hamilton was one of the boldest and most creative thinkers of his time. In sharp contrast to Jefferson, he supported the establishment of a strong federal government. He was a leader in the Federalist Party, and he believed that the U.S. Constitution should be interpreted loosely in order to give the federal government greater powers. Hamilton distrusted the common people and worked to protect the interests of merchants and other members of the business community.

Republicans feared a strong central government and a strong presidency. The party primarily represented small farmers, who were unenthusiastic about big cities, banks, and industry.

The differences between the parties had grown during the 1790s as a result of disagreements about Alexander Hamilton's program to strengthen the American economy, his proposal to create a national bank, the federal whiskey tax, and relations with Great Britain and France. The Federalists looked to Great Britain for friendship; the Democratic-Republicans looked to France.

The bitterness between the parties and the Federalists' fears about the Democratic-Republicans were also shown by Federalist support for the Sedition Act of 1798. This law permitted the government to prosecute anyone publishing "any false, scandalous and malicious writing" about the U.S. government, Congress, or the president. It was used to convict Democratic-Republican editors and printers who had criticized the Federalists, but it was so unpopular that it probably contributed to the defeat of the Federalists in the 1800 election.

During political campaigns these days, we are often concerned about "negative campaigning"— advertising in which a candidate tells what is wrong with the candidate of the other party. Plenty of negative advertising also took place back in 1800— though it was limited to newspapers, leaflets, and broadsides (a large sheet of paper printed only on one side). The Democratic-Republicans accused John Adams of favoring a monarchy, and they declared that only the "friends of war" would vote for Adams. The Federalists claimed that Jefferson didn't

Thomas Jefferson reading a draft of the Declaration of Independence, *left. Below,* the signers of the Declaration of Independence dipped their quills in this inkstand, made by silversmith Philip Syng, a friend of Benjamin Franklin's.

John Adams

believe in God, that he would destroy religion, that he was a fanatic and a coward, and that he too would bring about war. The divisiveness of the election of 1800 threatened the American experiment. No one knew whether the two parties could work together to keep the government functioning.

Another difficulty also surfaced during that election. In 1800 the system of electing the president differed in important ways from what it is now. Then, as now, presidential electors were chosen in each state. But now each elector casts one vote for president and one for vice president. In 1800 each elector cast two votes for president, and the candidate who received the most votes was elected president. The runner-up became vice president. The framers of the Constitution intended that the vice

Differences Between the Parties

FEDERALISTS		DEMOCRATIC-REPUBLICANS
Yes	Federal assumption of state debts	No
Yes	Creation of a Bank of the United States	No
Yes	Protective tariff	No
Yes	An aristocracy of wealth	No
Yes	Pro-British rather than pro-French	No
Yes	Use of implied powers	No
Yes	Alien and Sedition Acts	No

president be the second-best man for the presidency. Because he had finished second in 1796, Jefferson had become vice president—even though he was opposed to Adams's policies.

When the votes in the election of 1800 were counted, the Democratic-Republicans had won, but barely. The two Federalist candidates—President John Adams and Charles C. Pinckney—had a total of 65 and 64 electoral votes respectively. The two Democratic-Republican candidates—Thomas Jefferson and Aaron Burr—each had 73 electoral votes. According to the Constitution, the House of Representatives had to break the tie and decide who would be the next president. However, the Federalist Party still controlled the House. Each of the 16 states had one vote, and a majority (at least nine votes) was necessary to elect the president.

On February 11, 1801, just three weeks before John Adams was supposed to leave office, the representatives began voting. The Federalist congressmen voted for Burr against the advice of Alexander Hamilton, a leading Federalist. The Democratic-Republican congressmen all voted for Jefferson. After 35 ballots, neither man could secure a majority. Finally, the Federalists gave up. The next day Jefferson was elected on the 36th ballot with the votes of 10 states, and Burr became vice president.

The election of 1800 had shown a weakness in the Constitution. By the next presidential election, in 1804, the nation had ratified the 12th Amendment, which provided that each elector would vote separately for the president and the vice president, thereby preventing a tie between candidates of the same party.

In this cartoon from 1800, Federalists attacked Jefferson by showing the American eagle preventing him from burning the Constitution.

Life in 1801

W HEN THOMAS JEFFERSON BECAME president, the United States was a weak nation compared to the existing world powers.

The United States in 1801

The area covered by the United States was about one-quarter of what it is today. But the population—5,308,000—was one-fiftieth of what it is now. There was an average of six people for each square mile.

Fewer than half a million people lived in what was then called "the West"—the area from the Allegheny Mountains to the Mississippi River. Except for rare strips of land cultivated by isolated farmers, the West was almost completely forest. The year before Jefferson became president, a trav-

The president's house, now the White House, can be seen in the distant center in this view of Washington, D.C., in 1800.

eler named Thomas Ashe wrote of a night he spent in the Alleghenies:

> Darkness brought the din of the demons of the wood. Clouds of owls rose out of the valleys and flitted screaming about my head. The wolves, their howling reverberating from mountain to mountain, held some prey in chase, probably a deer.

That night Ashe said he heard "the noise of millions of little beings."

West of the Alleghenies, the only efficient way to travel was by water—on the Great Lakes or down the Ohio, Mississippi, or smaller rivers. It took 28 days for goods sent from Pittsburgh to reach New Orleans—the only port a westerner could use to send goods to the East Coast or to Europe. To return home up the Mississippi might take three months.

In the East, more than two-thirds of the population lived near the Atlantic seacoast, but here too the population was greatly spread out. Only 1 of every 25 Americans lived in places that could have been called cities (communities with more than 10,000 people). In 1801 the United States had five cities: Boston, New York, Philadelphia, Baltimore, and Charleston. Their streets were unpaved, undrained, unlit, and cluttered with garbage. Pigs ran free on many streets.

It is difficult to think of the United States as a unified country when Jefferson became president—not because of the divisions between the Federalists and the Democratic-Republicans, nor because of the differences between the North, the South, and the West. In 1801 there was no system of transportation

New England was the center of the shipbuilding industry, because of the demand there for fishing boats and merchant ships.

At this Boston shipyard, merchant ships were built for England as well as for the United States.

or communication to link a people scattered over hundreds of thousands of square miles. The only decent road in the country ran from Boston to New York to Philadelphia to Baltimore. The average speed on the road was 4 miles per hour, and it took three days to travel the 200 miles from Boston to New York. A heavy rain might make traveling impossible for days.

South of Baltimore, the roads became worse. When George Washington was president, his carriage got stuck in mud and had to be pried up with poles and pulled out by ropes. South of Washington, D.C., the roads were more like trails. In Virginia the roads were so bad that they were rarely used by coaches or wagons. Travel was usually by horseback. Virginia had many rivers, however. A few had bridges, and ferries operated on others. Still, when Jefferson was president, he had to cross four rivers and four streams to go from Monticello to Washington. Most

Travelers stop at an inn along the road from Baltimore, Maryland, to Washington, D.C. Stagecoaches provided the best transportation for passengers and mail in the 1700s and early 1800s.

BRITISH CANADA

PART OF MASS.

VERMONT

NEW HAMPSHIRE

MASSACHUSETTS

RHODE ISLAND

CONNECTICUT

NEW JERSEY

NEW YORK

PENNSYLVANIA

DELAWARE

MARYLAND

INDIANA TERRITORY

NORTHWEST TERRITORY

SPANISH LOUISIANA

VIRGINIA

KENTUCKY

TENNESSEE

NORTH CAROLINA

GEORGIA

SOUTH CAROLINA

MISSISSIPPI TERRITORY

Atlantic Ocean

SPANISH FLORIDA

The United States in 1801

Vermont became a state in 1791, Kentucky in 1792 and Tennessee in 1796. The Mississippi Territory was established in 1798. The Northwest Territory, created in 1785, was divided in 1800 when the Indiana Territory was established. The current Georgia border was established in 1802.

had neither bridges nor ferries, so he had to ford them alone on horseback.

In 1801 Americans were scattered over fields, forests, mountains, and swamps, and they could barely stay in touch with one another. The distances were vast, the people few.

Charles IV, shown here with his family, reigned as king of Spain during most of Jefferson's presidency.

The World in 1801

Most of the world was scarcely known to Americans in 1801. Australia had just begun to be colonized by Europeans, primarily the British. Except for slave traders, Africa south of the Sahara Desert was almost completely unknown to Americans. A small but steady trade with China was one of the few links Americans had with the continent of Asia. South America was part of the empires of Spain and Portugal.

For Americans in 1801, "the world" consisted of Europe and the rest of the North American continent—most of which had not yet been explored by Europeans. Only three other countries—Britain, France, and Spain—really mattered to Americans. Each owned a large part of North America, and each was an important world power.

Spain, which also claimed most of South America, was the weakest of the three countries. It owned what is now the state of Florida and a strip of land north of the Gulf of Mexico, which was then called West Florida. It also claimed the land that stretched from Texas to California. Spain had returned to France the Louisiana Territory, which it had received in 1762. This area stretched from Mexico in the south to Canada in the north, from the Mississippi River in the east to the Rocky Mountains in the west. Great Britain owned what is now Canada, and also claimed part of the Oregon Territory and some of northern Maine. None of these countries had reason to be permanently hostile to the United States, but each had interests opposed to those of the newly independent nation.

Americans warmly remembered how much France had helped the struggling colonies during the American Revolution. But that had been 20 years earlier, and much had happened since then. France, for example, had also undergone a revolution, a much more violent one than that of the American colonies. King Louis XVI, whose government had aided the colonies, had been overthrown in 1789. He and Queen Marie Antoinette had been executed. In 1801 France, led by Napoleon Bonaparte, threatened to conquer all of Europe. Only Great Britain stood

Much of the land in the United States was sparsely populated when Jefferson became president. This woodcut shows the vast wilderness between Wilmington, Delaware, and the Delaware River.

between Napoleon and the conquest of Europe. Between 1792 and 1815, Britain and France were almost continuously at war with each other.

Relations between the United States and Great Britain were not good either. Both sides thought the other had not fully lived up to the treaty of peace that had ended the American Revolution. Americans argued that the British had not evacuated forts in the American Northwest, as they had promised to do. The British pointed out that the United States had not paid old debts owed to British merchants, as they had agreed to do.

During this period, the United States also came close to war with Britain and France because of trade problems. The United States was neutral and traded with all nations, but the British began to seize U.S. ships carrying goods bound for France. They also boarded American ships to search for sailors who, they claimed, were British citizens and deserters from the British navy. When they found them, they removed them from the U.S. ship—a process called impressment—and forced them to work on British ships. A second war between the United States and Great Britain was prevented by a treaty negotiated in 1794 by Chief Justice John Jay. At the time, the Jay Treaty was extremely unpopular, because it appeared that the United States had given up much, while the British had given up little.

The United States also got into an undeclared war on the high seas with France. Beginning in 1797, the French government, angered by the Jay Treaty, began interfering with American shipping. The United States sent diplomats to France to negotiate a treaty of friendship and commerce, but they left

In 1794 more than 300 American ships had been seized by the British. Chief Justice John Jay, *above*, negotiated a treaty that ensured British evacuation from forts they still maintained in the Northwest Territory, but impressment did not stop. Many Federalists supported the treaty, but the Democratic-Republicans attacked it.

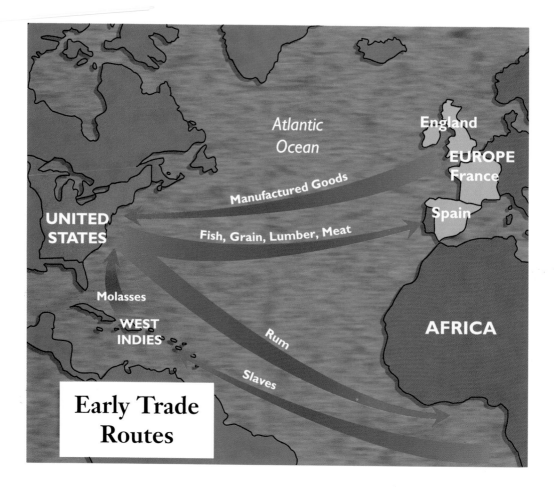

Early Trade Routes

in disgust after hints that there would be no negotiations unless the United States paid a bribe of
$204,000. When news of the situation (called the
XYZ Affair) reached the United States, the American people were outraged. The United States ended
its alliance with France, and the undeclared naval
war continued until 1800, when it was ended by the
Treaty of Montfortane.

When Jefferson became president, he was aware
that there might be danger both from the aggres-

George III, *left*, and George IV, *above*, ruled England during Jefferson's presidency.

In 1804 Napoleon Bonaparte crowned himself emperor of France. He was the greatest military genius of his time and one of the greatest generals in history.

sive France of Napoleon Bonaparte and from Great Britain, the world's greatest naval power. Neither country respected the United States as a world power. Only with Spain did relations appear to be satisfactory. By the Treaty of San Lorenzo, signed in 1795, Spain had recognized the borders of the United States and appeared to give Americans free navigation of the Mississippi.

Jefferson's Presidential Style

AS PRESIDENT, JEFFERSON SUC-ceeded two of his fellow patriots—George Washington and John Adams—men whose commitment to the American Revolution was as great as his own. Washington set an example for all later presidents (with the exception of Franklin Delano Roosevelt) by giving up power after two terms in office. Adams was a man of extraordinary character. Yet both Washington and Adams adopted a presidential style that seemed to many Americans too close in dress, ceremony, and etiquette to the royalty of Europe.

Washington had wanted the American people to think of their government as respectable and dignified. In public, Washington was aloof and formal. When he visited the Congress to give his State of

While Jefferson's elegant home reflects his character and special genius, his presidential style reflects his republican philosophy.

This 1801 portrait depicts Jefferson against a background of Virginia's Natural Bridge, a landmark south of Lexington. It symbolizes his fascination with the natural world.

In both New York and Philadelphia, President George Washington and his wife, Martha, entertained in an elaborate style. Martha held a formal reception every Friday night, but guests had to leave at 9:00 because the president liked to go to bed at that time. Fashionable gentlemen usually wore powdered wigs, for which they used the special gear shown below.

the Union address, he rode in a cream-colored coach drawn by six white horses. In front of him were two military aides on white horses. Behind him was another aide followed by carriages containing members of his cabinet. After Washington addressed them, members of Congress, like the British Parliament, rode in carriages the few blocks to the president's home to present him with a formal reply to his speech.

When Washington entertained, he held afternoon receptions, called levees, much like European royalty. Only important or wealthy people attended these receptions. Washington usually wore a black velvet coat, a white or peach-colored vest, knee breeches, and yellow gloves. His powdered hair was tied back. He held his military hat under his arm and carried a long sword in a green scabbard at his side. Washington did not shake hands with his visitors, but rather bowed to them. His dinners also were very

Jefferson felt that John Adams, *right*, had become much too fond of kingly rule and too distrustful of popular government. Like Washington, Adams and his wife, Abigail, enjoyed lavish, formal entertainment.

Candles were used as a source of light. They were extinguished with a candle snuffer, and wicks were trimmed regularly with a special wick trimmer.

large and formal, and guests were seated at a long table according to how important they were. If Washington's clothes, entertainment, and ceremonies seemed a bit elaborate in a government "for the people," it did fill a need for a head of state who seemed above name-calling and political deals.

As president, John Adams believed even more strongly than Washington that pomp and ceremony were necessary to maintain respect for the government. He even believed in long titles for government officials. As vice president, he had unsuccessfully tried to convince the Senate to refer to the president as "His Highness the President of the United States of America and Protector of the Rights of the Same."

Jefferson's style was completely different from that of Washington and Adams. From that first day as president, when he walked from his boardinghouse to his inauguration, Jefferson acted differently. He ended the levees and the formal dinners, he dressed informally, and he ignored titles. Although great balls had been given on the birthdays of Washington and Adams, Jefferson wouldn't even let anyone know the date of his birthday.

Instead of large, formal dinners at long tables, Jefferson invited about a dozen guests at a time to the White House. He used round tables rather than seating guests according to rank. In President Jefferson's house the rule was pell-mell—whoever got to the table first took the seat he or she wanted. To entertain as many people as he did, Jefferson paid 14 servants—including a French chef—out of his own income. One year his entertainment costs amounted to $16,000. Yet his salary as president was only $25,000 a year. By the time he left the White House, Jefferson's service as president had put him $11,000 in debt.

Twice a year—on New Year's Day and July 4th—Jefferson opened the White House to everyone. A military band played while Jefferson greeted everyone and invited them to have punch, cake, and other refreshments.

To deliver his State of the Union address, Jefferson simply put the speech in an envelope and had his private secretary deliver it to the Congress.

The U.S. five-cent piece, the nickel, features Thomas Jefferson on the front and Monticello on the back. *E pluribus unum* means "out of many, one." The Latin motto appears on other U.S. coins and on the Great Seal of the United States.

Jefferson was also more accessible to the members of his cabinet and the Congress. They were free to drop in at the White House in the morning without an appointment. He might, however, meet them in a threadbare coat, soiled shirt, and slippers. It is said that one senator who called to see him mistook him for the butler.

Occasionally, this behavior caused problems. For example, when the new British minister to the United States, Anthony Merry, paid a call on Jefferson, he was outraged:

> I, in my official costume, found myself at the hour of reception he had himself appointed, introduced to a man as president of the United States, not merely in an undress, but actually standing in slippers down at the heels, and both pantaloons, coat, and under-clothes indicative of utter slovenliness and indifference to appearances and in a state of negligence actually studied. I could not doubt that the whole scene was prepared and intended as an insult, not to me personally, but to the sovereign I represented.

*T*his 19-foot statue of Jefferson by the American sculptor Rudulph Evans stands inside the white marble Jefferson Memorial (shown on page 56), near the Potomac River in Washington, D.C.

Why was Jefferson's style as president so different from that of Washington and Adams? There are several reasons. First, Jefferson's personality differed from those of his two predecessors. Washington was a very formal, dignified man. Adams was a rather vain man, who enjoyed pomp and ceremony. Jefferson, though he had the polish of an aristocrat, was an informal man and a warm, natural host.

Jefferson also believed that if a big fuss was made about public leaders, they could eventually forget that they were responsible to the people—a situation that would not be good for either the people or the leaders. Jefferson believed that he could govern bet-

ter if he was open and accessible to people and their elected representatives. And Jefferson's style was very good politics. He gained great popularity by identifying himself with common people.

During the presidencies of Washington and Adams, the nation's capital had been located first in New York and then in Philadelphia. These were great cities by American standards. Many wealthy people had fine houses, and they held formal dinners and extravagant balls.

A portrait of Thomas Jefferson by Gilbert Stuart.

Washington, D.C.

*N*ine cities served as the national capital during the American Revolution through the establishment of the new government under the Constitution. The first capital for the new government under the Constitution (and the last under the Articles of Confederation) was New York City. The Constitution had provided that Congress would choose the site for the permanent capital, which could be no larger than 100 square miles, and that the area would be ceded to the national government by the state or states it was in.

Many places lobbied to be the national capital. Based on a political compromise worked out by Alexander Hamilton, James Madison, and Thomas Jefferson, the federal government moved to Philadelphia in 1790, and the temporary capital remained there until 1800. The perma-

nent capital was to be located on the Potomac River. President Washington chose the exact site, which was located not far from his great plantation, Mount Vernon. Maryland and Virginia gave the 100 square miles to the United States. (Fifty years later, the land on the Virginia side of the Potomac was returned to that state.)

The city was planned by a French engineer, Pierre L'Enfant, and laid out by Andrew Ellicott, an American surveyor. Both Washington and Jefferson closely supervised the building of the city. At the time the federal government moved to Washington—in the summer of 1800—only two government buildings had been constructed (neither was complete)—the Capitol (housing Congress) and the president's house (later called the White House). Only 14,000 people lived in the entire District of Columbia.

In the early 1800s, farm animals freely wandered the streets of Washington, D.C.

In 1800, however, John Adams moved to Washington, D.C., and became the first president to live in the White House, which was still unfinished. When Adams arrived in Washington, he found a village in the midst of a forest. Those who worked with government lived in one of two clusters—either near the Capitol or near the White House. Between the two, there was a single road—the only one in Washington—that ran through a wide swamp. When it was dry, riders on horseback raised great clouds of dust. When it rained, horses had to walk through oozing mud and through pools where mosquitoes, which carried malaria, bred. When Jefferson was president, Washington, D.C., had no sidewalks, no streetlamps, no road signs. One evening a congressman fell from his horse halfway between the White House and the Capitol. He wrote his wife that he was "almost bruised to death, on a dark, cold night, in the heart of the capital of the United States, out of sight or hearing of human habitation." The ceremonies of royalty would have looked very strange in such a place as Washington was then.

Jefferson was very fond of his daughter Martha, his oldest child. From France he sent her this locket with a miniature of her and this engraving: "Nobody in this world can make me so happy or so miserable, as you."

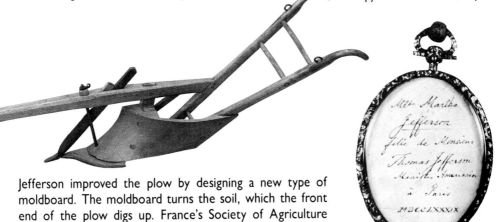

Jefferson improved the plow by designing a new type of moldboard. The moldboard turns the soil, which the front end of the plow digs up. France's Society of Agriculture awarded him a gold medal for his design.

Jefferson as President

*B*Y THE TIME JEFFERSON BECAME
president, he had made clear to his fellow
citizens the principles for which he believed
the Democratic-Republican Party stood. Upon those
principles he intended to govern.

His Political Principles

Jefferson gave no speeches when he ran for president
in 1800, and there were no national news services.
So how did he get his ideas to the people? In the
years before the election, he had spelled them out
in a series of letters to friends, party leaders, and
editors of newspapers friendly to the Democratic-

All, too, will bear in mind this sacred principle, that though the
will of the majority is in all cases to prevail, that will, to be rightful, must be reasonable; that the minority possess their equal
rights, which equal laws protect.

First Inaugural Address, March 4, 1801

Birth of Political Parties

Political parties were formed as the result of philosophical differences over the role of government, differences over policies, and because of personal ambition to hold public office. The Federalists, led by Alexander Hamilton, had their major support in the North among merchants and property owners, who favored policies to aid commerce and the growth of industry. The Federalists believed in a strong national government that would give active support to banking and shipping interests. They believed in close relations with England and doubted the ability of ordinary people to govern themselves.

An important part of the support for the Democratic-Republicans came from southern planters and northern farmers. The Democratic-Republicans were suspicious of banks, industry, and city life. They believed that the people could govern themselves through their elected representatives. They were concerned that the philosophy of the Federalists would make the central government so strong that it would threaten people's liberty. The Democratic-Republicans were sympathetic to the French and distrusted England.

These points of view could be seen in the differences between Thomas Jefferson and Alexander Hamilton, who both served in George Washington's first cabinet. Their differences increased as the result of bitter attacks from newspapers supporting each side. After Jefferson left Washington's cabinet on December 31, 1793, the Democratic-Republican position was not represented among Washington's close advisers. Out of power, Jefferson began building an organization that would support him in a race for the presidency. Differences between the parties grew as the result of the European war involving Great Britain and France, and Washington came under strong criticism from the Democratic-Republicans for his policies dealing with that war. The Federalists won the presidency in 1796 and controlled both houses of the Congress for most of the 1790s.

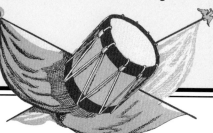

Republicans. Those letters were then shared with voters through local newspapers and leaflets. Jefferson repeated those principles in the speech he gave at his inauguration.

What were those principles? First, Jefferson believed in a government that would not cost too much—"rigorously frugal and simple" were his words. He believed in a government that would not use high taxes to "take from the mouth of labor the bread it had earned."

Thomas Jefferson

Jefferson did not believe that America needed a standing army or a large navy in peacetime because the country was so far from the quarreling nations of Europe. Jefferson hated spending money for defense, and he believed that a large defense budget would make war more likely. He wanted to keep America out of the quarrels of Europe. He was, he said, for "free commerce with all nations; a political connection with none."

Like most other American leaders in 1801, Jefferson was "a warm friend to the Constitution," but he disagreed with the way Federalists such as Alexander Hamilton had interpreted it. Jefferson thought that the Constitution left important powers to the states, but limited the powers of the national government so that it would not become so powerful as to encourage a monarchy and threaten freedom.

Alexander Hamilton

None of his ideas were new at the time Jefferson gave his inaugural address, but the eloquence of that speech was remarkable. In part, he called for:

> Equal and exact justice to all men, of whatever state or persuasion, religious or political; peace, commerce, and honest friendship with all nations, entangling alliances with none; the support of the State governments

in all their rights, as the most competent administration for our domestic concerns and the surest bulwarks against antirepublican tendencies; the preservation of the General Government in its whole constitutional vigor, as the sheet anchor of our peace and safety abroad; a well-disciplined militia, our best reliance in peace and for the first moments of war, till regulars may relieve them; the supremacy of the civil over the military authority; economy in the public expense, that labor may be lightly burdened; the honest payment of our debts and sacred preservation of the public faith.

In this speech, Jefferson stated one very important principle that helped dissolve the fears of those who had opposed his election. He said:

All, too, will bear in mind this sacred principle, that though the will of the majority is in all cases to prevail, that will, to be rightful, must be reasonable; that the minority possess equal rights, which equal laws protect.

An 1804 drawing of the president's house, now called the White House

In 1962 President John F. Kennedy gave a dinner at the White House in honor of Nobel Prize winners. Dozens of great physicists, chemists, writers, and government leaders were present. When he spoke to them, Kennedy said this:

I think this is the most extraordinary collection of talent, of human knowledge, that has ever been gathered together at the White House, with the possible exception of when Thomas Jefferson dined alone.

Then he added a few more sentences that did more than anything else to heal the wounds of the election and to heal the bitter split in American politics:

Every difference of opinion is not a difference of principle. We have called by different names brethren of the same principle. We are all republicans—we are all federalists.

Making Decisions

Many differences exist between Jefferson's world and ours. Jefferson had only one staff member, Captain Meriwether Lewis, to assist him, while now the president has hundreds of assistants. Since transportation and communications were so much slower in Jefferson's era than in ours, he had much more time to make decisions than the current president has. Now the president can get information from great libraries and computer databases. He can speak directly to experts on the telephone or fly them in for meetings. Jefferson had only his library and his mind. American presidents must now work with 14 executive departments, a Congress of 535 persons, and almost 200 foreign nations. In contrast, Jefferson only had to deal with about 140 members of Congress, 4 department heads, and no more than 12 foreign nations.

Because Jefferson traveled frequently, he wanted a comfortable way to write during his long trips. He designed this lap desk, which included a board to lean on while he wrote and a drawer to hold extra paper, pens, and ink.

Jefferson surrounded himself with intelligent men who were willing to disagree with him, and he encouraged his advisers to speak their minds. His secretary of state was James Madison, who is called the father of the U.S. Constitution because of his leading role in the Consitutional Convention. Jefferson's secretary of the treasury was an able Pennsylvanian named Albert Gallatin. Four of his cabinet members remained for all eight years of Jefferson's term—something that has never happened again.

In making decisions, Jefferson relied mainly upon his cabinet—the secretaries of state, treasury, war, and the navy—and his attorney general. Sometimes he asked for their opinions in writing. For major decisions, he usually met with the members of his cabinet. (The offices of his cabinet secretaries were in buildings on either side of the White House.)

When Jefferson asked for their advice, his cabinet members spoke freely in his presence. He did not want his advisers to tell him only what they thought he wanted to hear. Jefferson often wrote down the opinion of each cabinet member and often changed his policies after talking with them.

How did the president and the cabinet get the information upon which to base decisions in a time when there were no telephones, radios, or televisions? In Jefferson's case, much information came by mail. Jefferson was continually writing, receiving, and answering mail from his friends, Democratic-Republican Party leaders, and newspaper editors from all over the country. This was how he learned what was

In order to have a copy of the letters he sent, Jefferson used a device called a polygraph. This ingenious machine duplicated the writer's hand movements with a second pen on an adjacent sheet of paper.

Right, Secretary of State James Madison; *below*, Secretary of the Navy Robert Smith; *opposite page, from top to bottom*, Secretary of the Treasury Albert Gallatin, Attorney General Levi Lincoln, Secretary of War Henry Dearborn. John Breckinridge and Caesar Rodney also served as attorneys general.

happening and what people felt. He also explained his policies and decisions this way.

Jefferson wrote all his own letters—without a word processor, photocopier, or secretary. (He did have someone working in the White House called a "private secretary," but this person had nothing to do with the mail.) In his first year as president, Jefferson received 1,881 letters and wrote 677. He sometimes spent more than 10 hours a day at his writing desk, reading and answering mail.

President Jefferson also learned about what was happening throughout the country by talking with visitors to the White House and especially by talking with members of Congress. In fact, Jefferson stayed in close contact with members of Congress, and his "republican style" was useful in obtaining news. In contrast to the formality at the receptions of the first two presidents, at Jefferson's small dinners conversation flowed easily, and Jefferson could learn what was happening far from Washington.

Jefferson invited Federalist and Democratic-Republican members of Congress to these dinners—usually on different days. Sometimes, though, he didn't invite those congressmen who had bitterly attacked him. He also invited members of his cabinet, justices of the Supreme Court, and various diplomats—especially during the times when Congress was not in session.

When Congress was in session, Jefferson hosted dinners three times a week. This way he talked with many people. For example, between November 5, 1804, and February 22, 1805, Congress was in session for 110 days. During that period, Jefferson held 47 dinner parties, at which he entertained a grand total of 550 guests.

Jefferson tried to inform himself as best as he could about what the public was thinking, but he was not afraid to make decisions for which he might be criticized. He tried to remain open-minded enough to change his policy if it was not working. He also tried to remain faithful to what he believed the Constitution and his basic principles required.

Trade Money for Hostages?

ONE OF PRESIDENT JEFFERSON'S first important decisions was to use force rather than continue the standing policy of bribing North African rulers so they would not attack American ships. The way Jefferson dealt with this problem demonstrates how he asked for and listened to advice from his cabinet. It also shows how concerned he was about staying within the limits of the Constitution and how he modified his policies as a result of new information and new developments.

For many years, one of the most profitable businesses of Tripoli, Tunis, Algiers, and Morocco—the four North African states along the Barbary Coast of the Mediterranean Sea—was attacking foreign trading ships to demand tribute and ransom. The first American president to pay these pirates (known as the Barbary pirates) was George Washington. In

War with Tripoli, one of the Barbary States of northern Africa, began in 1801. During the war, the U.S. Navy bombarded Tripoli, *left*.

1793, 11 American merchant ships were captured by the dey (ruler) of Algiers, and 119 Americans were put in prison. At that time, the United States had no navy to fight the Barbary pirates, so Washington agreed to pay the dey $1 million to ransom the hostages and buy peace. The United States also gave the dey a personal gift of $540,000, agreed to provide ammunition and other arms, and promised to continue to pay Algiers twice a year. Soon after that, the United States made similar agreements with the bey of Tunis and the bashaw of Tripoli. By the time Jefferson became president, the United States had paid North African rulers approximately $10 million to protect the trade of about 100 ships a year. Ever since he had been U.S. minister to France, Jefferson had believed that such tribute was money wasted. As he said, "There is no end to the demand of these powers, nor any security in their promises."

Over the years, the United States had failed to keep up the payments. In 1800, when U.S. payments were three years behind, Algiers hijacked a U.S. ship, tore down its American flag, and forced it to sail to Constantinople. Just as Jefferson became president, cruisers from Tripoli attacked American ships. By this time, however, the United States had built a small navy—13 frigates, of which 6 were in service.

Jefferson wanted to use force against the Barbary states, but he had a problem. The Constitution makes the president the commander in chief of the army and the navy, but it gives Congress the power to declare war. What type of fighting could Jefferson order his captains to do without asking Congress to actually declare war? Jefferson called his cabinet together on May 15, 1801, to seek advice about what

In 1804 Lieutenant Stephen Decatur raided the port of Tripoli to set the frigate *Philadelphia* afire so it could not be used by the enemy. The frigate had been seized earlier by Tripoli.

orders he could give to the captains of U.S. naval vessels, while still abiding by the Constitution.

Jefferson had always worried about presidents becoming too powerful. He wanted to interpret the Constitution properly, so future presidents would have a precedent to follow. After listening to the differing views of his cabinet, Jefferson decided with the majority. The U.S. Navy could attack the ships of Tripoli, if Tripoli was found to be attacking American ships. Seven months later, when Jefferson gave his State of the Union address to Congress, he went further. He suggested that Congress authorize the navy to attack Tripoli's ships whenever it saw them, rather than waiting for them to attack first.

Congress refused to declare war against the North African states, but it did authorize the president to use the navy in whatever way he felt necessary to protect American seamen and commerce. Jefferson

The U.S. *Enterprise* attacked and captured the Tripolitan *Corsair* in 1801.

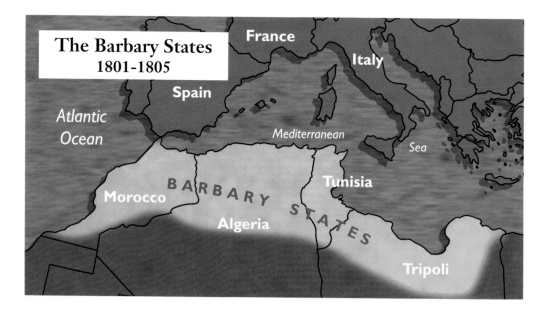

The Barbary States
1801-1805

France
Italy
Spain
Atlantic
Ocean
Mediterranean
Sea
Morocco
B A R B A R Y   S T A T E S
Tunisia
Algeria
Tripoli

sent more ships in 1802, but the naval commander was weak and lazy, and Jefferson had to fire him.

Jefferson chose a new commander, Commodore Edward Preble, who reached the Mediterranean just in time for the news that the U.S. frigate *Philadelphia* had run aground. It had been forced to surrender to Bashaw Yusuf Karamanli of Tripoli, and 307 Americans had been taken hostage. When Jefferson heard about this, he sent five more frigates. The United States now had six frigates, two brigs, and three schooners in the Mediterranean. Jefferson also replaced Preble with a more experienced commander, Captain Samuel Barron.

In the meantime, an American named William Eaton had made an agreement with Hamet Karamanli, the brother of the bashaw of Tripoli. The United States would pay for an expedition to overthrow the bashaw if Hamet, who would then become

During an attack on Tripoli, Lieutenant Stephen Decatur led a crew aboard a Tripolitan gunboat, *left.* The burning of the *Philadelphia, below*

the new bashaw, would sign a treaty of peace. Hamet would then become the new bashaw. Eaton built an army of 400 adventurers and soldiers of fortune, as well as seven U.S. marines. This little army crossed 500 miles of desert from Alexandria, Egypt, in

Modern-Day Hostages

*L*ike Jefferson, recent American presidents have also had difficulty preventing some Middle Eastern powers from taking American hostages and, once taken, in securing their release. President Jimmy Carter's inability to secure the release of 52 Americans held hostage in Iran in 1979 led to his defeat for reelection. The hostages were freed after a deal was made between the two countries, but not until after Carter left office.

President Reagan announced that his administration would never make deals with terrorists or terrorist nations for the release of hostages. In 1986, however, it became known that Reagan had authorized the sale of weapons

Ronald Reagan

to Iran to try to secure the release of hostages. Furthermore, it also became known that the money collected from the secret sale of the weapons had been secretly and illegally funneled by White House aides to the Nicaraguan Contras. The revelations damaged Reagan's reputation and made it difficult for him to govern during his last two years in office.

Thus, with Carter and Reagan, as well as with Jefferson, the greater military power of the United States was not helpful in securing the release of American hostages. While none of the three presidents wanted to deal with governments that tolerated pirates and terrorists, in the end all three had to pay some sort of ransom.

Opposite page, American hostages released from Iran during the Reagan administration.

March 1805. With the aid of three U.S. ships, it captured the city of Derna, Tripoli.

However, Jefferson thought this scheme might risk the lives of the 307 American hostages, so he sent a man named Tobias Lear, who had been George Washington's secretary, to negotiate directly with the bashaw. On June 10, 1805, Lear and the bashaw signed a treaty in which the U.S. agreed to pay $60,000 (much less than the original demand of $200,000) for the return of the hostages. The bashaw agreed that there would be no more annual payments from the United States. This was the best treaty any power had made with Tripoli up to that time.

Looked at one way, Jefferson's policy did not work. Just two years later, when the United States was close to war with Great Britain, the dey of Algiers broke the treaty, and the United States again paid tribute. Finally, in 1815, President James Madison sent two squadrons to the Barbary Coast. This time the dey, the bey, and the bashaw had to pay for a treaty with the United States! The U.S. Navy would continue to patrol the Barbary Coast for 15 more years.

By taking the position he did, Jefferson sent an important message to other nations—that the United States was not going to be taken advantage of. Jefferson was able to put forth this position without greatly increasing spending and without risking a war with a great power. Jefferson had also learned a lesson—that the United States had to spend some money on defense. It could not survive without a navy.

Jefferson was able to handle the Barbary rulers without assuming too much power as president. He placed responsibility for war where the Constitution had intended it to be—with Congress. But Congress had made an important decision as well. It gave the president the authority to use the navy to protect American seamen and commerce. Congress had found a way to allow the president to use his powers as commander in chief to protect the interests of the United States without having to declare war.

After the bombardment of Tripoli, a group of marines hauled down the Tripolitan flag and hoisted the U.S. flag.

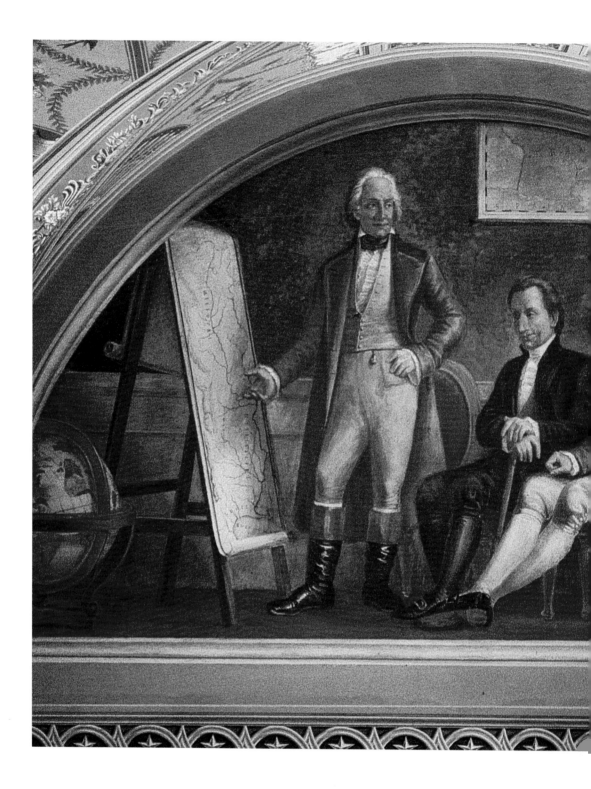

The Decision to Buy the Louisiana Territory

*T*HOMAS JEFFERSON'S MOST IM-
portant presidential decision was to buy
the Louisiana Territory from France. The
purchase of this land allowed the United States to
expand westward over much of the continent.

Actually, Jefferson only wanted to buy New
Orleans and what was then known as West Florida.
However, when Robert Livingston, the American
minister to France, tried to buy New Orleans, he
found that the entire Louisiana Territory (spreading
from the Mississippi River to the Rocky Mountains,
and from the Canadian border to the Gulf of Mexico) was for sale. Livingston made a deal, and Jefferson stuck by it. During this process, Jefferson
made three important decisions: first, to try to get

James Monroe and Roger Livingston were surprised when Napoleon, represented by Talleyrand, the French foreign minister,
offered to sell the entire Louisiana Territory.

Robert Livingston, *right,* who had helped draw up the Declaration of Independence, served as minister to France during Jefferson's first term as president. While in France, he negotiated the Louisiana Purchase.

Colonial currency

New Orleans peacefully by purchase; second, to stick with the deal to buy the entire Louisiana Territory, even though he was not sure that the Constitution gave the U.S. government power to acquire territory; and third, to send an expedition to explore the territory.

From 1762 to 1800, Spain had controlled the traffic on the Mississippi River. The Spanish owned the land west of the river and the city of New Orleans at its mouth. New Orleans was very important to those living in the American West, because it was the one port they could reach to sell their goods.

In 1795 Spain agreed to allow Americans to navigate freely on the Mississippi and to place goods on deposit in New Orleans. (The right to deposit meant the right to transfer cargo from riverboat to ocean vessel without paying a tax.)

But in 1800, Napoleon Bonaparte, who then controlled much of Europe, made a secret treaty with Spain. According to the terms of the treaty, Spain returned the Louisiana Territory to France—the former owner of the land. Jefferson was afraid that Napoleon might attempt to build an empire in America, as he had done in Europe. He believed that if Napoleon did this, the United States would become dependent on England for naval help, and he wrote, "From that moment we must marry ourselves to the British fleet and nation." Jefferson asked Livingston to warn the French that "[e]very eye in the United States is now fixed on this affair of Louisiana." He sternly told the French that "these circumstances rendered it impossible that France and the U.S. can continue long friends when they meet in so irritable a position."

While many of the Federalists were recommending that the United States take military action, Jefferson decided to see what he could do by negotiation. He told Livingston to try to buy the land on the lower Mississippi River or, if he couldn't do that, to get a clear promise of free navigation on the Mississippi as well as the right of deposit. A little while later, he asked his old friend James Monroe to join Livingston. Jefferson told Monroe that the

When James Monroe arrived in Paris in 1803, he urged Livingston to accept Napoleon's offer to sell the entire Louisiana Territory without waiting for Jefferson's permission. He then worked with Livingston to arrange the treaty. Jefferson was pleased with Monroe's initiative.

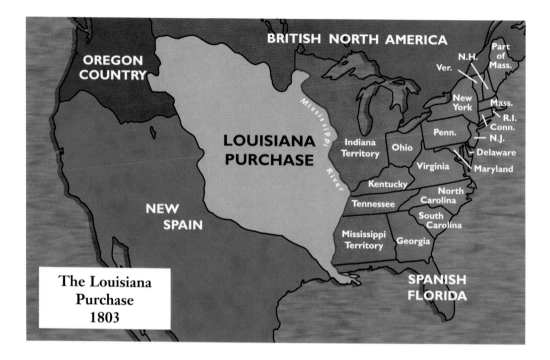

The Louisiana
Purchase
1803

The Louisiana Purchase doubled the area of the United States. This 1803 treaty with France extended the western U.S. boundary from the Mississippi River to the Rocky Mountains.

United States could pay approximately $9 million for New Orleans and West Florida.

On April 11, 1803—one day before Monroe reached Paris—Napoleon decided to try to sell all of the Louisiana Territory to the United States. We will never be sure why, but Napoleon had changed his mind about a French empire in America. Although briefly at peace with England, he expected war to begin again soon, and he needed money to fight it. Also, Napoleon thought that England might assist the United States in taking Louisiana by force. By selling the land, he could get money for his upcoming war in Europe.

Livingston met with Talleyrand (Charles Maurice de Talleyrand-Perigord), the French foreign minister, to discuss the sale. Livingston was shocked when

Talleyrand asked if the United States would be interested in buying the entire Louisiana Territory for $15,520,000. This was over $6 million more than the U.S. diplomats had the authority to spend. But Livingston, like just about everybody else, believed it to be a tremendous bargain. He and Monroe agreed to the purchase. The treaty was signed on May 2, 1803, and it reached Washington, D.C., on June 14.

This was the greatest real estate deal in U.S. history. The United States got 828,000 square miles

Napoleon Bonaparte

A ceremony honoring the Louisiana Purchase took place in New Orleans in 1803.

of land, an area bigger than all of western Europe. For about four cents an acre, the United States acquired the rich farmland of Iowa, Kansas, Arkansas, Missouri, the Dakotas, Nebraska, and Wyoming. It also received Minnesota and its great forests, Oklahoma and its oil, Montana and its copper, and the port of New Orleans. Most Americans were delighted by the deal, but some Federalists criticized it. One senator said, "It will be the greatest curse that could ever befall us."

After Jefferson heard the news of the purchase, he devoted his energies to getting Congress to ratify the treaty and appropriate the money to pay France. He was troubled because he could find nothing in the Constitution that clearly stated that the U.S. government had the power to acquire territory. As he stated it:

Part or all of 15 states were formed from the region that had been the Louisiana Territory.

> The general government has no powers but such as the Constitution has given it, and it has not given it a power of holding foreign territory and still less of incorporating it into the Union.

At first, Jefferson thought he would ask Congress for a constitutional amendment that would permit the United States to acquire land. That's what he had intended to do when he directed Livingston to buy New Orleans and West Florida. Passing a constitutional amendment, however, would be a slow process because—according to the Constitution—after two-thirds of each house of Congress votes for an amendment, three-fourths of the states must agree to it. Livingston and Monroe wanted the treaty approved quickly, before France could change its mind.

Napoleon shaking hands with Ambassadors Livingston and Monroe after signing the Louisiana Purchase treaty in Paris on May 2, 1803.

So Jefferson finally decided to take the view that the Federalists had always held: that the powers of the U.S. government are greater than those listed in the Constitution, because other powers are implied from those listed. The treaty was promptly ratified by Congress and the money appropriated. With the stroke of a pen, the United States doubled in size.

The purchase of the Louisiana Territory was one of the most important events in American history. At first, its importance seemed to be the increased movement of people into the area between the Alleghenies and the Mississippi. This movement was due in part to the fact that New Orleans had become a safe port to send goods. Also, the invention of the steamboat made the Mississippi one of the great highways in the world and New Orleans one of the great ports. The Louisiana Purchase was extremely popular. Congress gave an elaborate dinner to celebrate it, with Jefferson and his cabinet as honored guests. Jefferson's reelection as president was assured.

Talleyrand served as Napoleon's advisor and foreign minister.

The Decision to Explore

*J*EFFERSON MADE ONE OTHER important decision in regard to the Louisiana Territory. He decided to urge Congress to pay for an expedition to explore the territory, much of which was unknown to anyone except the Native Americans living there. He did so because he believed that the government ought to contribute to the spread of geographic and scientific knowledge. He also hoped to discover a water route across the United States to the Pacific Ocean.

Jefferson had been thinking of exploring the Missouri River Valley and the Rocky Mountains area for years. In 1802 he had asked the Spanish minister to the United States if his government

Jefferson had shown a great interest in the West for a long time. He obtained a grant from Congress for exploration of the region all the way to the Pacific Ocean. The Lewis and Clark expedition explored the vast wilderness of what is now the northwestern United States.

would object to such an expedition. Spain became suspicious of plans for American expansion and did object to the expedition. In 1803, before the Louisiana Territory was purchased, Jefferson had sent a secret message to Congress to request funding for a small expedition. To help convince Congress, Jefferson pointed out that such an expedition would increase the U.S. fur trade. Congress agreed, and passed the $2,500 appropriation.

Jefferson appointed Meriwether Lewis, a 29-year-old army captain, to command the expedition. Lewis had been Jefferson's private secretary, so he would be missed, but he knew the West. Lewis then asked William Clark, a 33-year-old army captain, to join him in leading the expedition. All this planning

This painting by Charles Morgenthaler depicts the start of the Lewis and Clark expedition at St. Charles, Missouri, in May 1804.

took place before word had reached Jefferson that the United States had signed the treaty with France to purchase the Louisiana Territory.

Lewis and Clark's memorable trip began on the Missouri River on a rainy Monday, May 14, 1804, near St. Louis, Missouri. Twenty-seven men went with them, and the expedition lasted almost two and a half years. Lewis and Clark arrived back in St. Louis on September 21, 1806. They had faced death dozens of times—crossing icy mountains, passing through roaring river rapids, and facing wild animals. They

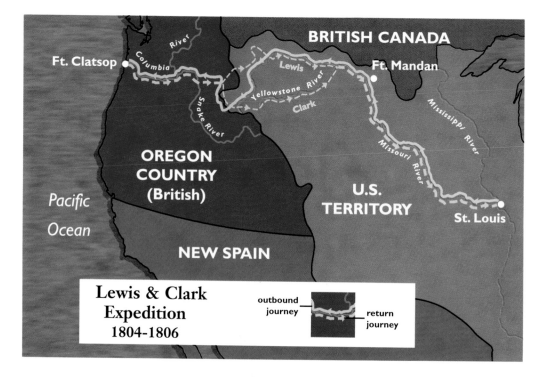

BRITISH CANADA
Ft. Clatsop
Columbia River
Lewis
Yellowstone River
Ft. Mandan
Clark
Snake River
Mississippi River
OREGON
COUNTRY
(British)
Pacific
Ocean
U.S.
TERRITORY
Missouri River
St. Louis
NEW SPAIN

Lewis & Clark
Expedition
1804-1806

outbound
journey
return
journey

A drawing of a salmon trout by William Clark from his journal for March 1806

had been tormented by violent cloudbursts, huge hailstones, hordes of mosquitoes, and thorns so sharp that they pierced the toughest moccasins. Although Lewis and Clark did not find a direct water route from the Missouri River to the Pacific Ocean, they did reach the Pacific. The explorers contributed greatly to scientific and geographic knowledge. They had "discovered" 122 species of animals and 178 species of plants. They also encountered 24 Native American tribes not previously known to Americans or Europeans. The Lewis and Clark expedition had shown the possibilities for trade and farming west of the Missouri. It made Americans look west and think of themselves not as a tiny country, but as a vast continent.

In what is now North Dakota, explorers Meriwether Lewis and William Clark hired a French Canadian trader named Toussaint Charbonneau as an interpreter. His wife, a Shoshone woman named Sacagawea (also spelled Sacajawea), joined the expedition as well. She aided in communication when the explorers reached Shosone territory in the Rocky Mountains.

Exploration Continues

*P*resident Jefferson had political, commerical, and scientific reasons for organizing the Lewis and Clark expedition. Costing only $2,500, the Lewis and Clark expedition was an epic of exploration, a milestone furthering American trade and settlement of the North American continent. The expedition brought back to a curious world information on weather, plants, animals, geographical features, and the customs of Native Americans.

Expeditions of the American space program have made similar contributions. The Mercury program to orbit the earth, the Apollo program to reach the moon, the Pioneer and Mariner programs to send probes to the planets, and the space shuttle brought back extraordinary information about the moon, the solar system, and the farther reaches of the universe, as well as information about how men and women can survive in space. While it is too early to know all the effects of the space program, like the Lewis and Clark Expedition it also had political importance, reinforcing America's position as the most technologically advanced nation in the world. Like the Lewis and Clark expedition, the space program has also had commercial importance, creating new projects and causing dramatic advances in communications. In time, the space program may, like the Lewis and Clark expedition, be seen as a milestone in opening up vast resources for development and advancing settlement of a new frontier.

Vehicles of exploration—almost two centuries apart

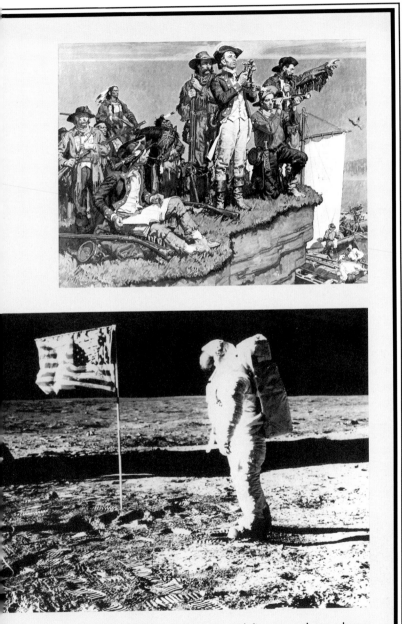

Instruments used for exploration and discovery, then and now

While in Montana, Lewis and Clark found many beavers. This discovery encouraged fur companies to build trading posts in the region. The soft, thick pelts of beavers were in demand because they could be made into stylish hats. The fur companies sent trappers called mountain men into the area. These men lived a rugged life, exploring wilderness known only to Native Americans.

The Decision to Try Aaron Burr for Treason

*A*NOTHER OF JEFFERSON'S DECI-sions involves one of the strangest stories in American history—and one of the strangest characters. Americans often think of Aaron Burr as a villain, because he killed Alexander Hamilton in a duel. But he may also have been a traitor. Jefferson certainly thought so.

In 1807 Aaron Burr was 51 years old. Born in New Jersey, he was a Revolutionary War hero, and he had served on George Washington's staff. After the Revolution, Burr became a lawyer and an important politician in New York. He could be considered the first American professional politician, because he knew far better than anyone of his time how to run a political campaign.

The trial of Aaron Burr for treason in Richmond, Virginia, drew thousands of people to the city.

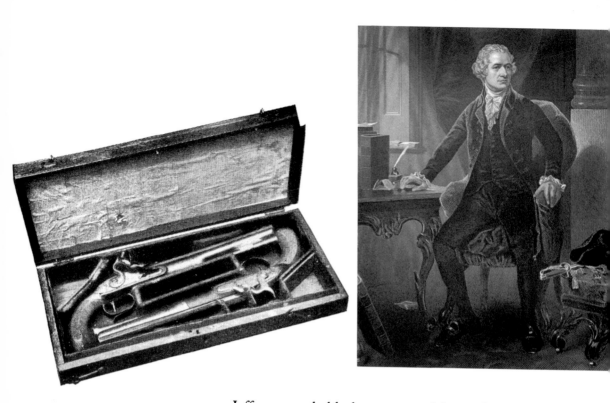

The pistols used by Alexander Hamilton and Aaron Burr in their 1804 duel, *above*. Hamilton is shown, *above right*, in a painting by Alonzo Chappel.

Jefferson probably became suspicious of Burr after the electoral vote in 1800. When the votes were counted, Jefferson and Burr were tied. Jefferson expected Burr to withdraw in Jefferson's favor, but he did not. Soon after that experience, Jefferson began to view Burr as a rival and refused to help him in any way. Jefferson did not want Burr to be his running mate in 1804, and the Democratic-Republicans nominated Governor George Clinton of New York for vice president. Burr then ran for governor of New York but was defeated—mainly because of attacks by Alexander Hamilton. Those attacks led to the duel on July 11, 1804, in which Burr killed Hamilton. Although Burr was still vice president, he had to flee New York to escape being arrested for murder. His political career seemed over.

Burr's conduct in 1805 and 1806 led many people to think that he was involved in a dangerous conspiracy. He held secret meetings with the British

Election of 1804

*I*n sharp contrast to the close election of 1800, Jefferson was reelected easily in 1804. That election was the first to take place after the ratification of the 12th Amendment to the Constitution, provided for separate balloting for president and vice president.

Having dropped Aaron Burr as his running mate, Jefferson chose another New Yorker, seven-term governor George Clinton. President Jefferson, an effective leader of his party, increased Democratic-Republican strength by his policies and appointments. With the nation prosperous and at peace, Jefferson was very popular. The Federalists had no issue to use effectively against the Democratic-Republicans.

Running against a ticket of Charles Cotesworth Pinckney of South Carolina and Rufus King of New York, both Jefferson and Clinton won in a landslide by 162 electoral votes to 14. Pinckney and King were only able to win the states of Connecticut and Delaware and two electoral votes from Maryland.

Thomas Jefferson

George Clinton

A Democratic-Republican placard of 1804 urging the election of Jefferson and Clinton

The duel between Hamilton and Burr was fought at 7:00 A.M. on a grassy ledge above the Hudson River, at Weehawken, New Jersey. Standing 10 paces apart, they waited for the signal to fire. Burr took deliberate aim, but Hamilton's was a random shot. Hamilton, wounded in the side, died the next day.

minister to the United States, and he was in contact with the government of Spain. He traveled through the West—down the Ohio and Mississippi Rivers—and met with several important people. One of the people he saw was General James Wilkinson, governor of Upper Louisiana. Wilkinson was a crafty man who was secretly receiving payments from Spanish officials for providing them with information about the United States.

Some people thought Burr was plotting to establish an empire of his own, an independent nation west of the Mississippi River. Other people believed he was trying to get the people who lived in the Spanish colonies to rebel. Still others thought he was preparing to lead an army to conquer Mexico. Jefferson heard those rumors in 1805 and early 1806, but he did not take them seriously.

However, in the late summer of 1806, Burr stayed on an island in the Ohio River. Blennerhassett Island was owned by Harman Blennerhassett, a friend of Burr's. This island became the center of operations for an expedition Burr was organizing. Men were being recruited, boats were being built, but the purpose of all the activity was unclear to everyone except those involved.

General James Wilkinson was instrumental in the arrest of Aaron Burr.

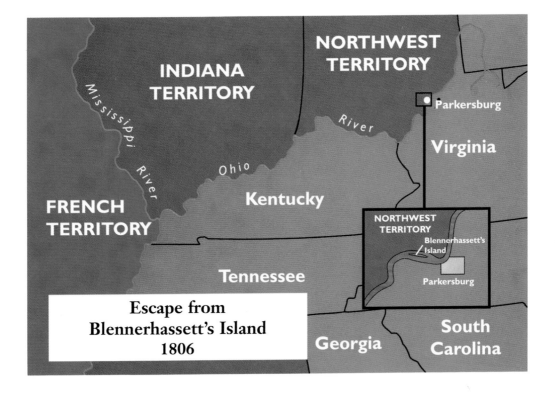

Escape from Blennerhassett's Island 1806

Harman Blennerhassett provided Burr with a center of operations to develop his plan.

Jefferson became concerned about Burr's plans in October 1806, when he received reports about Burr's activities. Jefferson began to worry about the southern part of the Louisiana Territory, which was surrounded by Spanish troops on land and open to British attack from the sea. Jefferson met with his cabinet, and they decided that the governments of the western states would have Burr "strictly watched and, on his committing any overt act unequivocally, to have him tried for treason, misdemeanor, or whatever other offense" he might have committed.

In November Jefferson received a letter from the wily Wilkinson. Enclosed in Wilkinson's letter was another letter, unsigned, stating that the operation was beginning and that the writer and his men would meet Wilkinson in Natchez, a city along the Mississippi River.

We do not know if Burr wrote that unsigned letter, but Wilkinson wanted Jefferson to think so—and Jefferson did. On December 9, a group of men acting under the orders of Ohio governor Edward Tiffin seized 10 boats on the Ohio River. Shortly after that, a local militia planned to seize the boats and men on Blennerhassett Island, but Blennerhassett and his men escaped by sailing down the Ohio River, which empties into the Mississippi.

Jefferson met with his cabinet and then determined that Burr was leading a treasonous conspiracy and was therefore a traitor to his country. Once Jefferson was convinced of Burr's guilt, he decided to act and became almost obsessed with destroying the conspiracy. Jefferson issued a proclamation for all government officials to arrest anybody involved in the alleged conspiracy. On January 22, 1807, Jeffer-

Thomas Jefferson, *left*, sent Congress a message accusing Burr of treason.

The seal Jefferson used on his letters

son sent a special message to Congress in which he accused Burr of being the "prime mover" in a conspiracy to sever the Union and attack Mexico. He stated that Burr's "guilt is placed beyond question."

With Jefferson's encouragement, General Wilkinson had many of Burr's followers arrested and imprisoned without a warrant. Jefferson, the apostle of liberty, wrote to W. C. C. Claiborne, governor of Orleans Territory, that "on great occasions every good officer must be ready to risk himself in going beyond the strict line of the law, when the public preservation requires it. ... The...opposition will try to make something of the infringement of liberty by the military arrest and deportation of citizens, but if it does not go beyond such offenders as...Burr, Blennerhassett,...etc., they will be supported by the public approbation."

Burr was arrested and taken to Richmond, Virginia, to be tried for treason. He was accused of bringing together an armed force in order to seize New Orleans, cause a revolution in the Orleans Territory, and separate the western states from the United States. We cannot be sure whether it was Jefferson's fear for the Union or his political rivalry with Burr that caused him to consider Burr guilty before the trial took place—which made it very difficult for Burr to have a fair trial.

Burr's trial was an important event in the history of Richmond. The city's population of 5,000 doubled. Eloquent gentlemen from Boston, delicate southern belles, and rough mountain men came to witness the trial. Taverns were full to bursting. Many people slept in tents or wagons, or on riverbanks. Everyone who was anyone seemed to be at the trial. Four men who had or would become U.S. attorneys general were among the lawyers. Three future governors of Virginia sat on the grand jury, and the witnesses included Andrew Jackson, who would become the seventh president of the United States.

Burr stood trial for treason before Chief Justice John Marshall and Judge Cyrus Griffin. Marshall did not like or trust Jefferson, and Jefferson felt the same about Marshall. Early in the trial, Burr asked

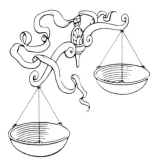

The scale of justice

Richmond, Virginia, *left,* was filled to capacity during the trial of Aaron Burr. *Below,* the state capitol, located in Richmond, was designed by Thomas Jefferson.

Marshall to issue a subpoena (a court order demanding designated documents or evidence) for Wilkinson's letter about Burr's plans. This act raised an important constitutional question: Could a judge order the president of the United States to provide evidence at a trial? Jefferson was angry about the subpoena. He refused to turn over the entire letter to Marshall, but did recopy the letter, omitting parts that he said were not about the alleged treason. Marshall chose to accept what Jefferson did, but he indicated that the choice was his—not Jefferson's—to make.

As the presiding judge, Marshall controlled the admission of evidence. The case was not clear-cut, and Marshall was in a position to prevent anything that he regarded as a miscarriage of justice. Marshall wanted to make it extremely difficult for treason to be used as a tool against political enemies, and he refused to admit certain evidence against Burr on the

Chief Justice John Marshall raised the Supreme Court to a level equal to the executive
and legislative branches of government.

grounds that it was irrelevant. Also, the Constitution provided that "no person shall be convicted of treason unless on the testimony of two witnesses to the same overt act, or on confession in open court." Wilkinson, who turned out to be a weak witness, testified against Burr. Blennerhassett, however, refused to testify against him. As a result, the jury found Burr not guilty of treason. Jefferson was furious. He

We shall never know for sure whether Aaron Burr, *left*, was guilty of treason. Andrew Jackson, *above*, was a witness at the trial. He later became the seventh president of the United States.

The Burr Trial and the Watergate Case

*I*n 1974, 167 years after the Burr trial, the Supreme Court had to consider a contention similar to that made by President Jefferson. The case of *United States v. Nixon* (the case of the Watergate tapes), one of the most important cases ever decided by the Supreme Court. It again raised the question of whether the president could refuse to turn over information to a court.

The case involved the scandal that had begun with a burglary of Democratic Party campaign headquarters in the Watergate Apartment complex in Washington, D.C. The burglars, who were caught in the midst of their crime, were linked to the White House and to some of President Richard Nixon's closest aides. The trail of evidence seemed to run to Nixon himself. When it became known that Nixon had made tape recordings of conversations in his office, a special prosecutor tried to obtain the tapes related to the burglary for use in the criminal trial of Nixon's aides. The prosecutor

Richard M. Nixon

believed the tapes might establish the truth or falsity of Nixon's denial that he had had anything to do with the burglary or the cover-up attempt.

Nixon refused to turn over the tapes, claiming—as Jefferson did—that the president was protected by "executive privilege" and did not have to turn over confidential information to a court. Jefferson, of course, was not the subject of a criminal investigation, and he did turn over most of the Wilkinson letter to the court.

The Supreme Court agreed in part with Nixon, saying that most of the time a contention by the president that information is privileged should be respected by the courts. But the Supreme Court also held that in a criminal proceeding, the need to protect the system of criminal justice outweighed the needs of the president. When Nixon made public the particular tapes the special prosecutor had subpoenaed, there was enough damaging evidence to lead to his resignation from office.

claimed that "it now appears we have no law but the will of the judge." Burr fled to Europe for a few years and then returned to New York, where he practiced law until he died in 1835.

We will never be quite sure what Aaron Burr was up to in the West. If Burr was trying to commit treason, then Jefferson's action helped prevent it. Even if that was not Burr's intention, it was reasonable to arrest Burr and bring him to trial. Jefferson, however, should not have declared to the nation that Burr was guilty in advance of the trial, nor should he have condoned Wilkinson's violations of civil liberties, nor should he have worked so single-mindedly for Burr's conviction. The Burr trial symbolized a growing rift in the Democratic-Republican Party. One faction believed that it was better to endanger the precepts of government than to violate the civil liberties of a single individual. The other faction felt that in the interest of preserving the liberty of the majority of people, individual liberties must occasionally be sacrificed. Jefferson generally thought of himself as part of the first group, but during the alleged Burr conspiracy, he slipped into the second group.

The U.S. Supreme Court building

The Decision to Establish an Embargo

*N*OT EVERY DECISION A PRESI-
dent makes will be a wise one. Like anyone else, presidents make mistakes, and
Jefferson was no exception. In 1807 he decided to
establish an embargo (a law stopping all trade with
another nation) against Great Britain. He did this
in an effort to prevent Great Britain from interfering with U.S. ships. The embargo divided the
country and did not change Great Britain's behavior.
Worse, when it became clear that the policy was
failing and was unpopular, Jefferson clung even more
firmly to it.

At this time in Europe, Napoleon Bonaparte had
become the emperor of France. He was at the height

When the British frigate *Leopard* opened fire on the U.S. frigate
Chesapeake on June 22, 1807, Jefferson had to decide how the
United States would respond. He later wrote: "The affair of the
Chesapeake put war into my hand. I had only to open it and let
havoc loose."

*J*efferson named James Monroe, *above,* minister to Great Britain. He asked Monroe to negotiate a trade treaty and instructed him to seek an indemnity for the ship seizures and impressments as well as a regularization of trade practices. Monroe was able to gain some concessions on trade but not on impressment. In 1806 Monroe helped conclude a treaty that was so unsatisfactory that Jefferson refused to submit it to the Senate. Britain (and France) continued to interfere with American shipping and to commit outrages against American crews.

of his power, but England and France were once again at war. Although Napoleon controlled most of Europe, Great Britain's navy was too large and powerful for Napoleon to invade England. The war between England and France became deadlocked, and each country tried to deprive the other of the material means of waging war. Each tried to block ships carrying goods and supplies to the other. Napoleon announced his intention to seize all neutral ships bound to or from a British port. The British, in turn, announced that they would blockade all French ports.

Americans were caught in the middle. The United States, a neutral nation, had hundreds of merchant ships carrying goods, but hardly any navy to defend them. As a result, many U.S. ships were seized. Since Great Britain had a bigger and stronger navy than France, more U.S. ships were seized by Britain than by France.

The British also began stopping American ships and coming aboard to search for sailors who, they said, had once been British sailors, and who were still British citizens. If they found any, they took them off U.S. ships by force. However, thousands of Americans were also seized and forced into the British navy. This policy, called impressment, greatly angered Americans.

Relations between England and the United States became increasingly tense, and any small incident might have caused a war. Then, on June 22, 1807, the British frigate *Leopard* hailed the U.S. frigate *Chesapeake* a few miles from the coast of Virginia. The British commander demanded the surrender of 4 men on the *Chesapeake* who he said were deserters. When the American commander refused to allow

British sailors frequently boarded American ships to search for sailors they claimed had deserted the British navy. Because it was difficult to tell a British seaman from an American, the British often seized Americans and forced them to serve in the British navy, a policy known as impressment.

the British to search his ship, the British opened fire, killing 3 men and wounding 18. The 4 "deserters" were taken from the *Chesapeake*. When Americans heard about the incident, most felt ready for war.

An angry Jefferson called his cabinet together. He was faced with four choices: negotiate, go to war, establish an embargo, or do nothing and submit to Britain. After four cabinet meetings, he decided to order all British ships out of U.S. ports, prepare for war, and call Congress into special session. In the meantime, he hoped that through negotiation the British would apologize for the incident and end impressment.

When negotiations with Great Britain failed, Jefferson had to decide what to do next. After another

A wharf in Salem, Massachusetts, after the Embargo Act went into effect. Forbidden to leave American ports, ships were tied up and left idle here and at other wharves for more than a year.

cabinet meeting Jefferson decided to avoid war. Against the advice of Secretary of the Treasury Albert Gallatin, he recommended that Congress pass a law imposing an embargo. Congress did so, and the Embargo Act became law on December 22, 1807. The Embargo Act made it illegal for U.S. ships to leave for foreign ports. No American goods could be sent to Europe. In addition, some British goods were not allowed to be sold in the United States. Jefferson thought that cutting off all U.S. trade would badly hurt both England and France, because they wouldn't receive the goods and supplies they needed. He also hoped the embargo would force Great Britain to stop attacking U.S. ships.

Except for some shipowners, most Americans initially supported Jefferson and the embargo, but they misjudged the world's dependence on the United

States. Ultimately, the embargo was a disaster. In a single year, U.S. exports dropped 80 percent. Some Americans broke the law by smuggling goods across the Canadian border or the border with Spanish Florida, but for 14 months most U.S. ships stayed in port. Cargoes rotted in harbors. Sailors and shipbuilders were unemployed. Some smaller seaports such as New Haven, Connecticut, were ruined. Americans became divided in their view of the blockade, and many in New York and New England turned bitterly against it. Meanwhile, the British and Canadian shipping industries thrived, because they replaced the United States in trade with South America. Neither Britain nor France changed their policy of stopping U.S. ships.

The embargo might have been worth trying for a while, but Jefferson's big mistake was in not ending

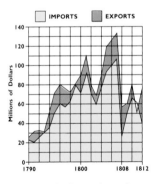

This graph shows how drastically trade fell during the embargo.

This cartoon shows Jefferson trying to calm those who strongly opposed the Embargo Act.

it when he saw it was not working. He also erred in not explaining to the American people that the embargo was an attempt to find a peaceful substitute for war. Instead, Jefferson spent much of his time and energy trying to make the embargo more effective. For example, the government had to pass additional laws to increase the nation's coastal defenses and to enforce the embargo. Jefferson found himself favoring more and more federal control—thus acting against his own principles about limiting the power of government, and especially that of the president. Jefferson would not end the embargo, in spite of economic decline, political losses for the Democratic-Republicans, and growing public discord.

Two Stubborn Presidents

Thomas Jefferson

Lyndon B. Johnson

*J*efferson's handling of the embargo was, in some ways, like Lyndon Johnson's continuation of the Vietnam War 160 years later. Each man took his policy so personally that he would not listen to criticism. Each held to his policy long after it became clear that it was failing and losing public support.

He had become a prisoner of his own policy. Finally, three days before he left office, Jefferson signed a law ending the embargo. His last year and a half as president had been unhappy and unsuccessful.

The Last Years
1809-1826

*J*EFFERSON WAS MORE THAN ready to leave the presidency when his second term as president ended on March 4, 1809. It is said that while he was attending the ball given in honor of his successor, James Madison, someone said to Jefferson, "You have now resigned a heavy burden." Jefferson supposedly replied, "Yes, indeed, and I am much happier at this moment than my friend [Madison]."

Had Jefferson left office at the end of his first term, he would have received little but praise for his accomplishments. At the end of his second term, however, he had to count some failures. The most serious one was the embargo policy, but there were others. He had hoped to see a constitutional amend-

When Jefferson returned to Monticello, he enjoyed the company of his daughter, Martha, her husband, Thomas Mann Randolph, and their seven children. Three more grandchildren were born later.

ment that would have given the federal government the power to help build canals and roads, aid science, and create universities. He did not accomplish those things. Finally, as a result of the embargo policy, he left his friend Madison with a divided country and a divided party.

Jefferson's achievements were many, and he took pride in the purchase of the Louisiana Territory and the Lewis and Clark expedition. His most important achievement, however, was showing the American people that a change in power from one political party to another may mean a change in policies, but it does not mean revolution or suppression of the other party.

Jefferson was the first president to show that it was possible for a president to be the leader of one political party while representing all the American people. He had been so successful in building the Democratic-Republican Party and converting Federalists that he was reelected in 1804 by a huge margin: Jefferson got 162 electoral votes, compared to Federalist candidate Charles C. Pinckney's 14 votes. Jefferson was also successful in being a strong leader of Congress, while still respecting the importance and independence of that body.

Throughout Jefferson's two terms, the United States was at peace, except for the skirmishes on the Barbary Coast. As he promised, Jefferson cut the debt owed by the U.S. government—from $83 million to $57 million, and he did this while reducing taxes. As he said in his second inaugural address, "It may be the pleasure and pride of an American to ask, what farmer, what laborer, ever sees a tax gatherer of the United States?"

Jefferson's friend James Madison was elected president in 1808 and took office in March 1809.

Not the least of Jefferson's achievements was his decision not to run for a third term. In spite of the unpopularity of the embargo policy, Jefferson could probably have had his party's nomination and won reelection fairly easily. However, he had always feared that the presidency might become a lifetime position, more like that of a king. He believed that to leave office at the proper time was as much a duty as to faithfully execute the office, and—following Washington's example—that is what he did.

Jefferson was almost 66 when he left the presidency. He never returned to Washington but lived the rest of his life at Monticello, where he was surrounded by a large family. His only living daughter, Martha, was there when he returned. So was his son-in-law, Thomas Mann Randolph, and seven of their children. Three more grandchildren were born later.

Thomas Jefferson Randolph, *left,* and Cornelia Randolph, *right,* were two of the grandchildren that lived with Jefferson at Monticello. Jefferson's daughter, Martha, is pictured in the center.

Scenes from Monticello include Jefferson's bed, *above,* from which he could enter either his study or his bedroom—depending on which side he rose from; the garden and orchards, *below;* the dining room and an invitation to dinner, *opposite page.*

Wine grapes and apricots are two of the fruits Jefferson introduced into the United States because of his interest in farming and plants. He also brought the olive tree, *bottom,* to America.

After the British attacked and burned much of Washington, *right,* Jefferson sold the books in his personal library at Monticello to rebuild the Library of Congress.

During these years, Jefferson spent much time supervising his plantations. Owning more than 10,000 acres, he raised sheep and grew wheat and tobacco. But he was more than a farmer. He also made and sold nails, and he owned two waterwheels, one of which he used to process the grain of other farmers. He also manufactured cloth—linen, cotton, and wool.

After the British set fire to the Capitol during the War of 1812, Jefferson sold his personal library of 6,500 books to rebuild the Library of Congress. Ten wagons were needed to take the books to Washington. But that did not stop him from buying more books—he collected more than 2,300 books before he died. Much of Jefferson's time in his later years was spent reading.

At the age of 70, Jefferson started a new project—building the University of Virginia, America's first state university. Jefferson, more than anyone else, convinced the Virginia legislature to pay for the school. He decided the subjects to be taught, the schedule of classes, and the rules of student conduct. Jefferson also designed the campus of the university as an "academical village" with buildings containing classrooms, rooms for students, and houses for professors. Covered walkways connected all the structures. His design was unlike any other U.S. campuses of that time—most of which were in a single building.

Later, Jefferson added to his plans the rotunda, a large building with a dome, to house the university library. In August 1824, when the Marquis de Lafayette visited America and came to Monticello, Jefferson used the rotunda to give a banquet for his old friend. Jefferson thought that founding the university was one of his greatest accomplishments.

After his presidency, Thomas Jefferson renewed his close friendship with John Adams, *above*, through letters. The University of Virginia, designed by Jefferson, is seen below.

Jefferson designed this swivel chair, footrest, and pivot-top writing desk, *right and below.* The swivel allowed him to turn around if someone came in to talk to him.

Perhaps the most wonderful thing about the last years of this remarkable man was the rebirth of his friendship with John Adams. They never saw each other again in their later years, but when they overcame the walls built by the political battles of the 1790s, they wrote each other often and seemed to think about each other even more often. This correspondence was precious to them both.

What interesting letters they wrote—about politics, the history they had made together, religion, science, the books that they were reading, and being a great-grandfather. Adams wrote that "when-

At Monticello in 1821, the 78-year-old statesman sat for his last-known portrait, by artist Thomas Sully. Even at this late date, only five years before his death, the former governor, secretary of state, vice president, and president witnessed the fulfillment of yet another major accomplishment—the opening of the University of Virginia, which he designed and founded.

ever I sit down to write you so many subjects crowd upon me that I know not what to begin." Jefferson wrote that of the many things he knew, "none more surely that I love you with all my heart, and pray for the continuance of your life until you shall have tired of it yourself."

Lafayette made a triumphant tour of the United States and went to Monticello to see his old friend Thomas Jefferson. "Teach your children to be as you are," Jefferson wrote Lafayette, "a cement between our two nations." A U.S. postage stamp honoring Lafayette is shown below.

LANDING OF GEN. LA FAYETTE
At Castle Garden, New York,
16th August 1824.

Entered According to Act of Congress the 27th Day of October 1824 by Samuel Maverick of the State of New York

Is My Country the Better for My Having Lived at All?

Sometime before he became president, Thomas Jefferson sat down one day and wrote: "I have sometimes asked myself whether my country is the better for my having lived at all?" He answered, "I do not know that it is." He then listed 11 things he had accomplished. He included the Declaration of Independence, but he also listed sending some olive plants from France to South Carolina and Georgia, where they were flourishing. Jefferson thought that the same things would have been done by someone else, if he had not lived, and he thought some of them might have been done "perhaps, a little better."

He was a modest man, but perhaps no American

has ever had more talents or accomplished as much as Jefferson. The Declaration of Independence, the Virginia Statute for Religious Liberty, creation of the first national political party, the unification of the country after the election of 1800, the purchase of the Louisiana Territory, and the Lewis and Clark expedition make up some of his political accomplishments. He also designed beautiful buildings and created innovative inventions.

More than any other person, Jefferson understood and wrote beautifully about what was and what could be special about the United States. Jefferson understood the opportunity the United States had to affect freedom all over the world. At a time when the United States was essentially the only free, democratic nation in the world (and not even all Americans were free then), Jefferson knew that if America succeeded, people in other countries would have a greater hope for freedom. By the way he talked and wrote about his belief in the peoples' ability to govern themselves, in equality, in freedom of expression, and in tolerance for all religions, Jefferson set the standard not only for his time but for the entire future of the country. He was not the only person to have such goals for our country, but he was one of the most important, and he wrote about them more eloquently than any American ever has. That is why his country is so much the better for his having lived at all.

Thomas Jefferson's telescope

July 4, 1826, was a day of joy throughout the United States. People celebrated the 50th anniversary of American independence with festivities throughout the country—picnics, parades, booming cannons, and speeches.

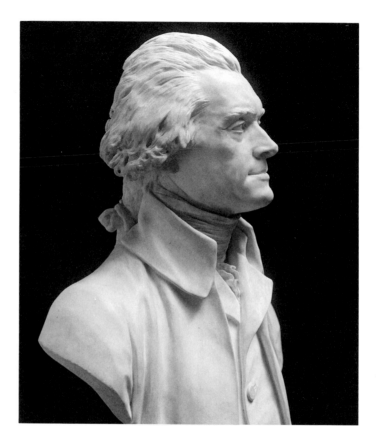

A marble bust of Thomas Jefferson by French sculptor Jean Antoine Houdon

The two old friends who had the most to do with writing the American Declaration were too ill to attend the celebrations. John Adams was 90. Thomas Jefferson was 83. A few weeks before, both men had sent messages explaining their absence. Jefferson was still writing with his old eloquence: "All eyes are opened or opening to the rights of man." At 10 minutes before 1:00 on the afternoon of July 4th, Jefferson died at Monticello. A little less than an hour before, the dying Adams had uttered his last words, "Thomas Jefferson still survives."

Even now that remains true.

Index

Acknowledgments

Albemarle Convention & Visitors Bureau, 118 (center); American Philosophical Society, 123; Amherst College, 114; Architect of the Capital, 74-75, 116 (top); Bettmann, 41, 45, 90-91; Bettmann Archive, 45 (sidebar, both), 65 (top), 81 (sidebar), 99 (sidebar); Boston Athenaeum, 15 (bottom); Bowdoin College Museum of Art, Brunswick, Maine, 53; California Apricot Advisory Board, 119 (sidebar, top); John D. Cunningham, Visuals Unlimited, 119 (sidebar, bottom); Delaware Art Museum, 33; Diplomatic Reception Rooms, United States Department of State, 55 (sidebar), 98; Print & Picture Collection, the Free Library of Philadelphia, 88 (left); Historical Society of Pennsylvania, 27, 30-31; Independence Historical National Park, 6-7, 27 (sidebar, both), 33, 101 (sidebar); Independent Picture Service, 26 (sidebar), 32, 34 (sidebar), 43, 50, 51, 64, 76, 92 (right), 97, 103 (bottom), 120 (sidebar); Jefferson Memorial Foundation, 23 (sidebar), 55, 62, 63, 110, 112-113, 115 (right and left), 119 (bottom), 121; John F. Kennedy Library, 61; The Library Company of Philadelphia, 35 (top); Library of Congress, 12-13, 20, 25, 26, 28, 36-37, 39, 42, 46-47, 49, 54, 64 (sidebar), 65 (center and bottom), 77, 95 (sidebar), 96, 106, 115 (center), 117 (bottom); Louisiana State Museum, 79; Mansell Collection, 79 (sidebar); Mariners Museum, 71 (bottom); James Marrinan, 76 (sidebar); Maryland Historical Society, 16, 93 (left); Minnesota Democratic Farm-Labor Party, 111 (right); Missouri Historical Society, 86 (sidebar); Montana Historical Society, 89 (sidebar); Museum of Fine Arts, Boston, 124; National Aeronautics and Space Administration (NASA), 88 (right), 89 (bottom); National Archives, 68, 69, 73 (top), 117 (sidebar); National Gallery of Art, Art Resource, Washington, D.C., 59 (bottom); National Portrait Gallery, 59; New Jersey Historical Society, 15 (top); New York Historical Society, 101; New York Public Library, 92 (left), 94, 120 (Stokes Collection); North Wind Picture Archives, 99; Oregon Historical Society, 89 (top); Peabody Essex Museum, 108-109; Bryan Peterson, 87; Jim Schwabel, 52, 56-57, 124; Kevin Shields / New England Stock Photo, 22, 118 (bottom); Smithsonian Institution, Museum of American History, 62; State Historical Society of Missouri, Columbia, 84; State Historical Society of North Dakota, 82-83, 85 (both); the Supreme Court Historical Society, 103 (sidebar); UPI / Bettmann, 73 (bottom); U.S. Navy, 71 (top), 66-67; Virginia Division of Tourism, 119 (top), 22 (inset), 122 (top); Virginia Historical Society, 23; Virginia Museum of Fine Arts, 9; Welches, 119 (sidebar, center); the White House, 72, 102; White House Historical Association, 111 (left); Yale University Art Gallery, 18-19.